GW01340100

Hayes

rewind

This has always felt like the most enjoyable and satisfying job in the world. We are in a privileged position where we are allowed a glimpse of the future before it happens.

This book is a thank you to everyone who has contributed to what we do and a celebration of an adventure. A passion for art, architecture and technology forged in art classes, architecture colleges and architecture practices, combined with contributions from Fiji to Los Angeles, Edinburgh, Sydney and London has led to over 5,000 images, 120 hours of video, 50,000 days work by the team, countless cups of tea and coffee, great parties, and more fun than we ever imagined.

If illustration fuels the transition of dreams into reality, then the computer has provided rocket fuel. Ink drawings we drew by hand over wireframe images in 1989 have in the last ten years been superseded by our development of still, photomontage and video scenes where Hollywood software merges the real and the virtual, and where beauty, programming and information combine to create complex interactive scenes. This continues to be an incredibly exciting time to experiment and develop our work in such a powerful emerging medium. We relish the opportunities that the application of new technology allows us in the future.

Architectural illustration is at its most powerful when the energy and enthusiasm of a strong architectural idea is translated with emotion into images. Our inspiration has come from architects, designers, artists, photographers and most of all from the giants of architectural illustration. A real love of architecture and building shines strongly in the stunningly evocative works of Cyril Farey, Hugh Ferris, William Walcott and Gordon Cullen. Impact, power, strength, perspective, composition and balance are all beyond technology.

A special thanks is reserved for our friends who have helped, inspired and supported us. Carlos Diniz, everyone at RRP, Andreas Whittam Smith, Ben Johnson, Laurie Abbott, Simon Smithson, Nacho Germade, Peter Crowther, Anne Davidson, Donald Grahame, The Architecture Foundation, Lynne Bryant, Desmond Banks, Erica Bolton, Jane Quinn, Ken Hawkins, Ian McIntyre, Michael Royde, Yuli Toh, David Driver, Carrie Byles, Chris Wilkinson, Jim Eyre, Neil Bingham, Bob Hayes, Jonny Stopford, and to photographers Richard Davies, Nick Wood, Simon Hazelgrove and John Maclean whose outstanding work is behind the success of so many of our images.

Most of all my thanks go to the brilliant team at Hayes Davidson and fellow Directors Robert Gordon Clark, Alex Morris, Andrew Hilton and Stephen Whitton, as well as to Bim Daser whose unfailing support, patience and skill helped give Hayes Davidson a successful start in life.

Alan Davidson

contents

Tate Modern, Bankside
Dusk view from St. Paul's.
Design: Herzog & de Meuron.
1997

Somerset House
Courtyard view.
Design: Dixon Jones.
2000

Tate Britain, Millbank
Cross section.
Design: John Miller and Partners.
1999

Royal Opera House
Floral Hall at night.
Design: Dixon Jones.
1999

St. Botolph's House
Ground floor section.
Developer: Minerva Plc.
Design: Nicholas Grimshaw
& Partners.
2000

**Seoul Broadcasting
Corporation Korea**
Design: Richard Rogers Partnership.
1996

**Grand Union Building,
Paddington Basin**
View above A40.
Developer: Chelsfield Plc.
Design: Richard Rogers Partnership.
2001

Number One Poultry
Design: Stirling Wilford.
1996

One London Wall
Developer: Hammerson and Kajima.
Design: Foster & Partners.
2000

City Modelling Study
Client: Corporation of London.
1999

One London Wall
Detail.
Developer: Hammerson and Kajima.
Design: Foster & Partners.
2000

**The Point,
Paddington Basin**
View from canal.
Developer: Chelsfield Plc.
Design: Terry Farell & Partners.
1999

The Heron Tower
Dusk view from Waterloo Bridge.
Developer: Heron Property.
Design: Kohn Pederson Fox.
2001

Tate Modern, Bankside
Gallery view.
Design: Herzog & de Meuron.
1997

90 High Holborn
Dusk view.
Developer: Minerva Plc.
Design: Gensler.
2001

120 Fleet Street
Night view.
Design: Hurley Robertson.
1997

Fenchurch Street Tower
View from Waterloo Bridge.
Developer: Churchill Properties.
Design: Wilkinson Eyre.
2000

National Portrait Gallery
Cross section.
Design: Dixon Jones.
1999

Angel of the North
Design: Anthony Gormley.
1997

Swiss Re.
Dusk view.
Design: Foster & Partners.
1999

Number One Poultry
View from east.
Design: Stirling Wilford.
1996

Sainsburys
View from Blackfriars Road South.
Developer: Stanhope Plc.
Design: Foster & Partners.
2001

The Dome, Greenwich
Aerial view.
Design: Richard Rogers Partnership.
1998

St. Botolph's House
Aerial view.
Developer: Minerva Plc.
Design: Nicholas Grimshaw
& Partners.
1999

The Millennium Tower
View from South Bank.
Developer: Trafalgar House /
Kvaerner.
Design: Foster & Partners.
1998

50 Finsbury Square
Cross section.
Developer: Standard Life.
Design: Foster & Partners.
1998

The Dome, Greenwich
Body Zone.
Design: Branson Coates.
1998

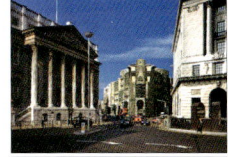

The Heron Tower
View from Bishopsgate.
Developer: Heron Property.
Design: Kohn Pederson Fox.
2001

The Heron Tower
View from Gracechurch Street.
Developer: Heron Property.
Design: Kohn Pederson Fox.
2001

The Heron Tower
View from Gracechurch Street
(detail).
Developer: Heron Property.
Design: Kohn Pederson Fox.
2001

Potsdamer Platz, Berlin
Night view: entrance.
Design: Richard Rogers Partnership.
1995

Old Broad Street
Night view.
Developer: CrossRail.
Design: Wilkinson Eyre.
1993

Aldgate Union
Reception view.
Developer: Tishman Speyer.
Design: Wilkinson Eyre.
2001

Brindley Place, Birmingham
Atrium view.
Design: Stanton Williams.
1997

**White City Shopping Centre
Shepherds Bush**
Mall interior.
Developer: Stanhope Plc.
Design: Ian Ritchie Architects.
1998

**Study for 3D map of the South Bank,
London.**
1997

280 Bishopsgate
Facade (detail).
Developer: Hammerson.
Design: Foggo Associates.
2000

280 Bishopsgate
Plaza (detail).
Developer: Hammerson.
Design: Foggo Associates.
2000

Arena Central, Birmingham
Developer: Hampton Trust.
Design: HOK.
1997

Tel Aviv
Masterplan proposal.
Design: Richard Rogers Partnership.
1997

88 Wood Street
Design: Richard Rogers Partnership.
1999

Albion Riverside
View from Cheyne Walk.
Developer: Hutchison Whampoa.
Design: Foster & Partners.
2001

Albion Riverside
Facade (detail).
Developer: Hutchison Whampoa.
Design: Foster & Partners.
2001

Albion Riverside
Night view looking east.
Developer: Hutchison Whampoa.
Design: Foster & Partners.
2001

Albion Riverside
Entrance (detail).
Developer: Hutchison Whampoa.
Design: Foster & Partners.
2001

Pierhead Lock
View from Thames.
Design: Goddard Manton.
1996

Montevetro
Facade (detail).
Developer: Taylor Woodrow.
Design: Richard Rogers Partnership.
1996

**Fulham Football Club
Redevelopment**
Aerial view.
Design: Snell Associates.
2000

Stratford Station
Elevational perspective.
Design: Wilkinson Eyre.
1995

Stratford Market Depot
Aerial view (detail).
Design: Wilkinson Eyre.
1991

Antwerp Law Courts
Competition view.
Design: Richard Rogers Partnership.
1998

South Quay Bridge
Aerial view (night).
Design: Wilkinson Eyre.
1994

Manchester Stadium Proposal
Aerial view (night).
Design: Arup Associates.
1999

Sainsburys, Greenwich
Aerial view (night).
Design: Chetwood Associates.
1998

Selfridges Birmingham
Facade detail.
Design: Future Systems.
2000

Hungerford Bridge
View from South Bank.
Design: Lifshutz Davidson.
1999

Loch Lomond Footbridge
Day view.
Design: Flint & Neill.
1997

Proposal for Singapore University
Design: Edward Cullinan Architects.
2000

Selfridges redevelopment
View from proposed restaurant.
Design: Foster & Partners.
2002

Saitama Stadium, Japan
Competition entry.
Night view.
Design: Richard Rogers Partnership.
1995

Lord's Media Stand
View from the stands.
Design: Future Systems.
1995

London Eye
View from Victoria Tower.
Design: Marks Barfield Architects.
1996

'Fast Forward'
London: a film about the future.
Hayes Davidson.
2001

London: 2050
Hayes Davidson.
1996

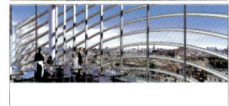

The Earth Centre
Design: Future Systems.
1997

Prado Museum, Spain
Design: Fosters & Partners.
1996

Chep Lap Kok Airport, Hong Kong
Design: Foster & Partners.
1997

Proposal for the Welsh Assembly
Aerial view.
Design: Richard Rogers Partnership.
1999

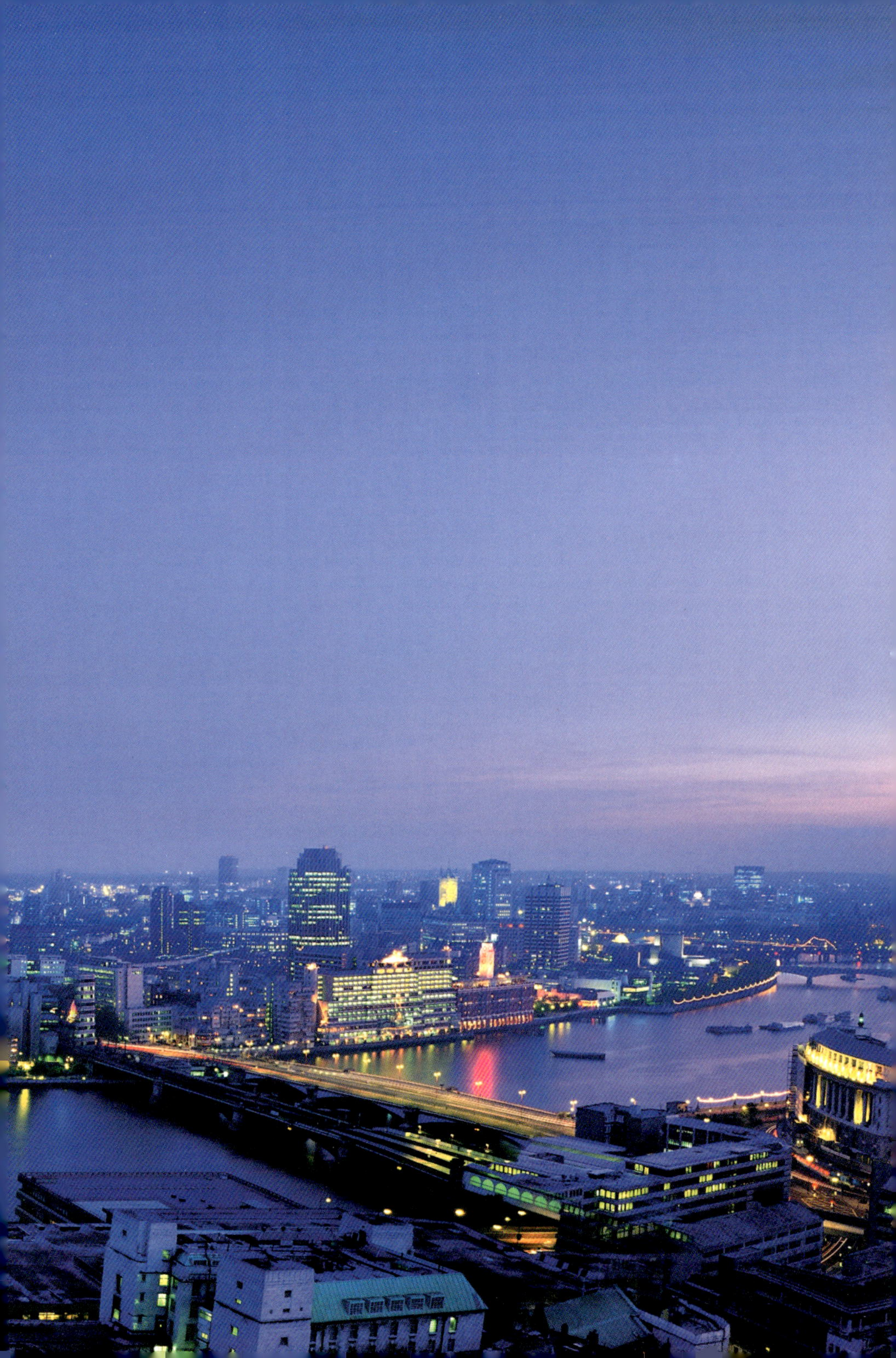

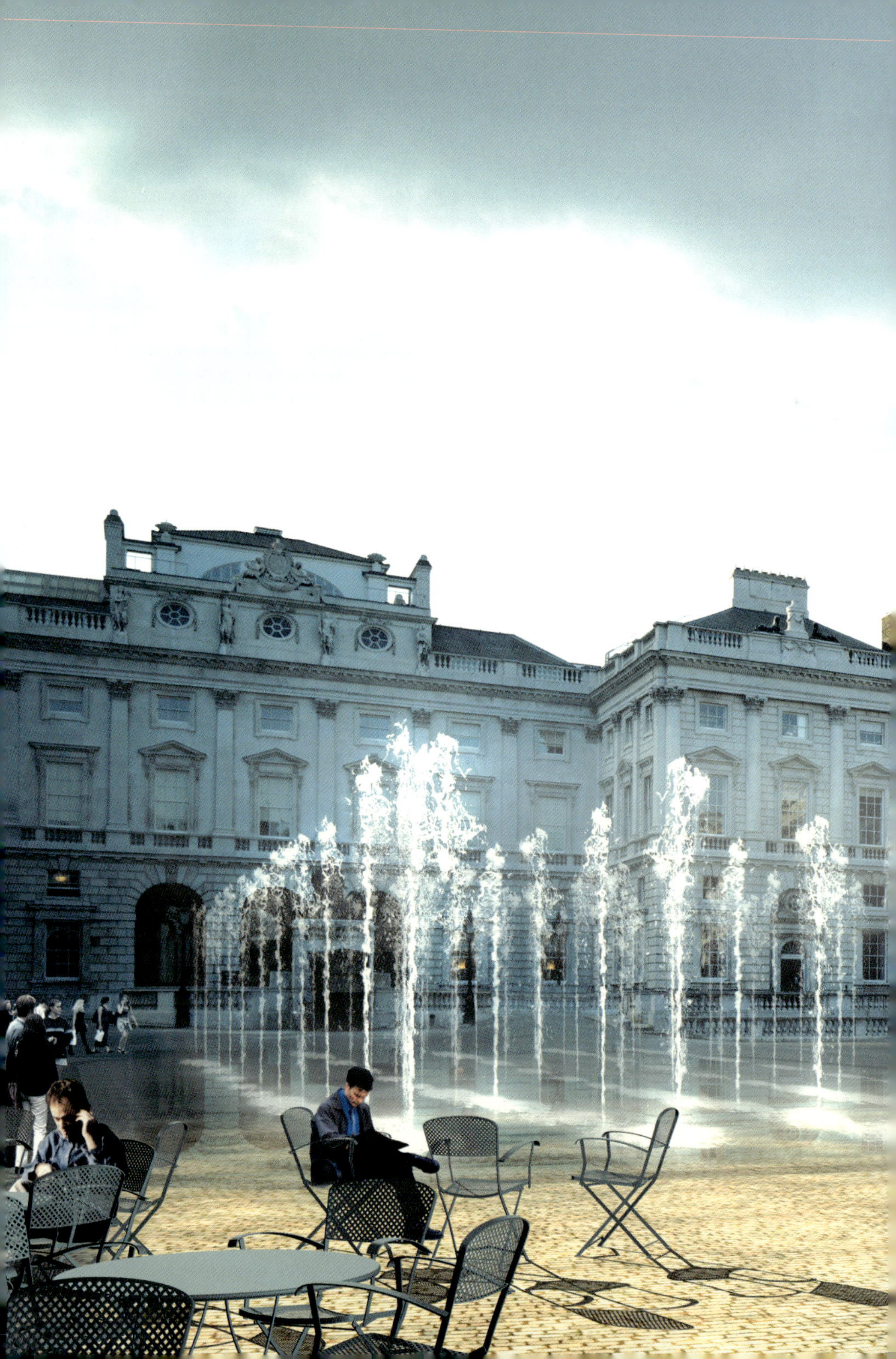

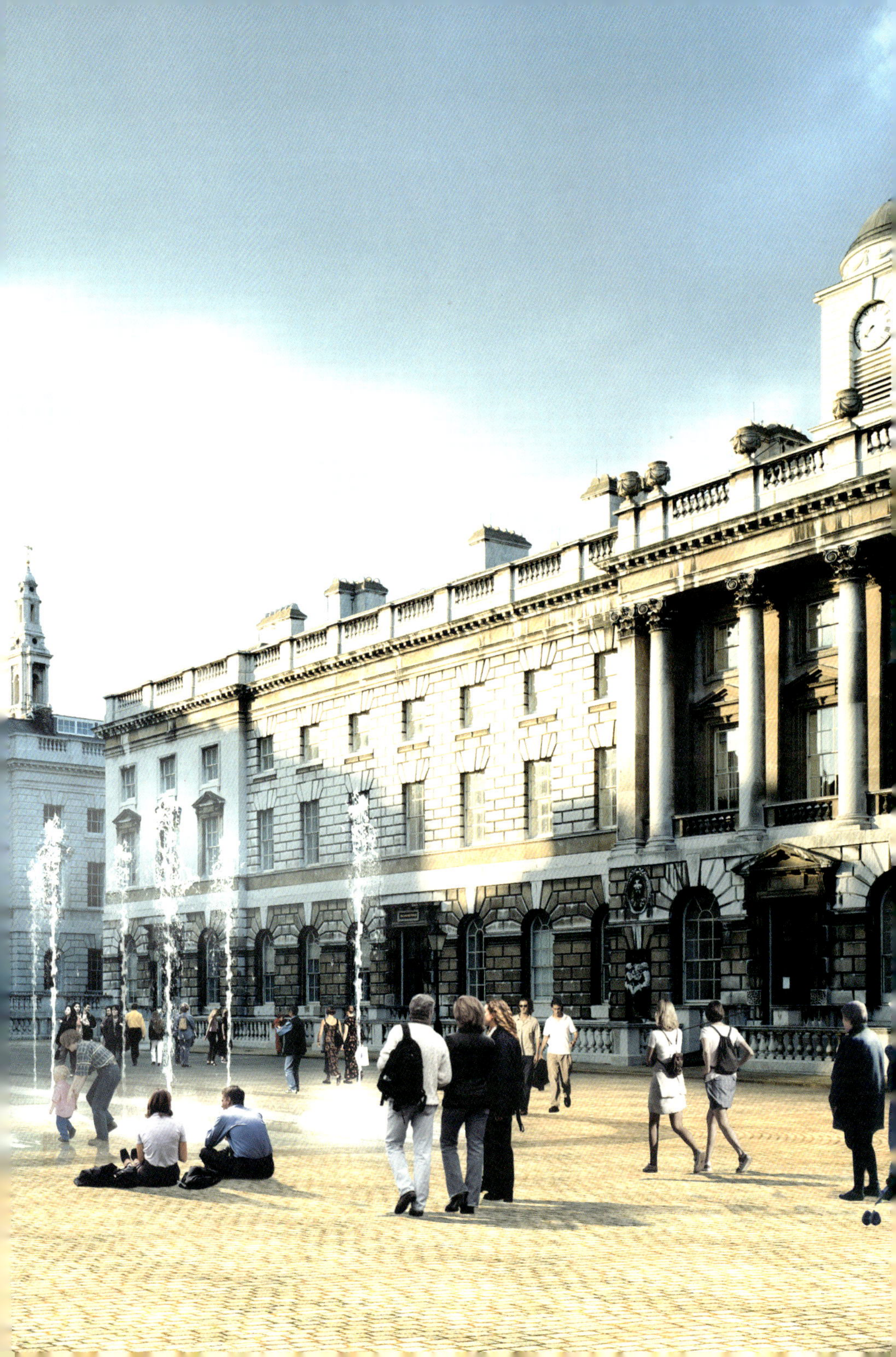

The existing Duveen Galleries

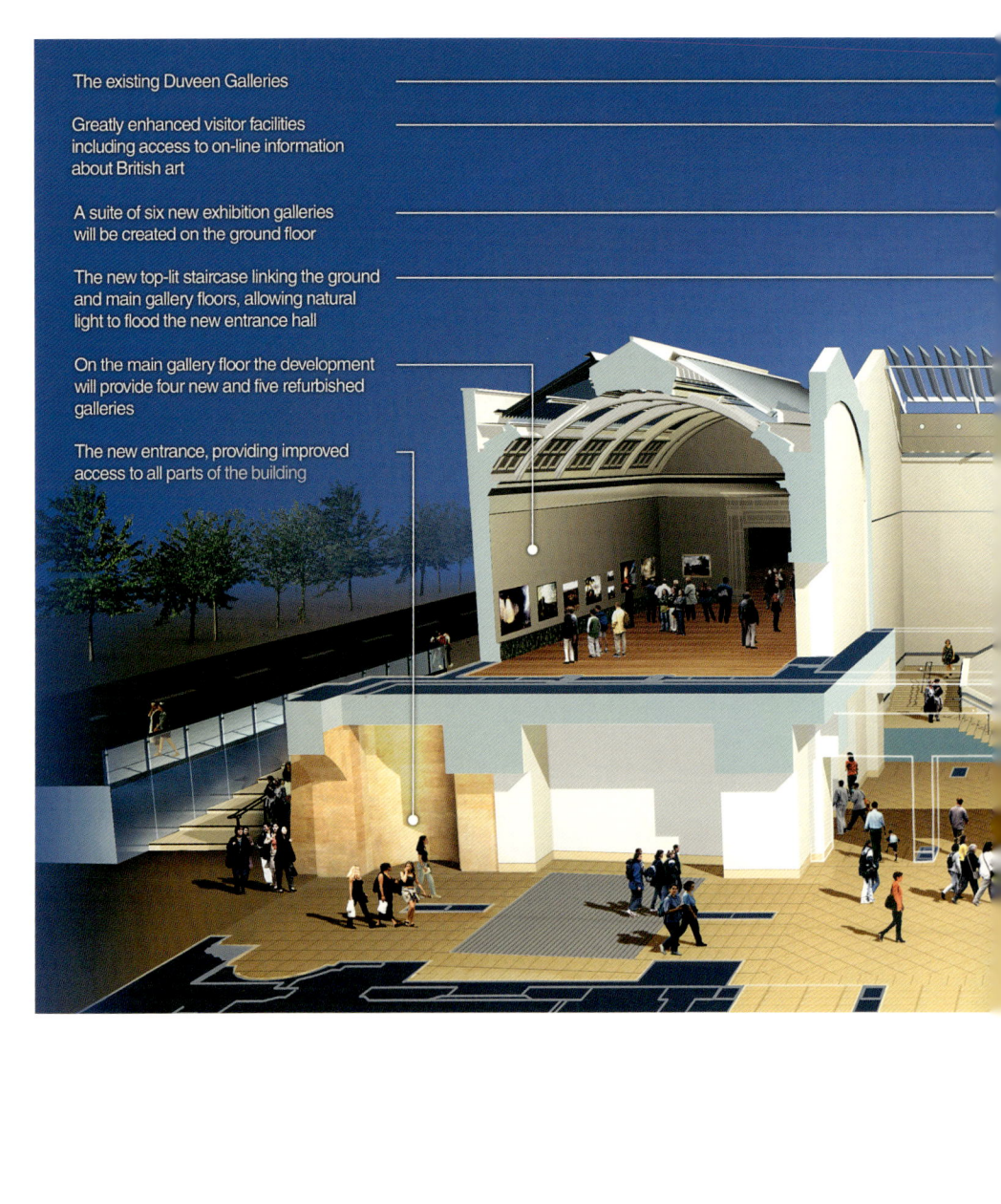

Greatly enhanced visitor facilities including access to on-line information about British art

A suite of six new exhibition galleries will be created on the ground floor

The new top-lit staircase linking the ground and main gallery floors, allowing natural light to flood the new entrance hall

On the main gallery floor the development will provide four new and five refurbished galleries

The new entrance, providing improved access to all parts of the building

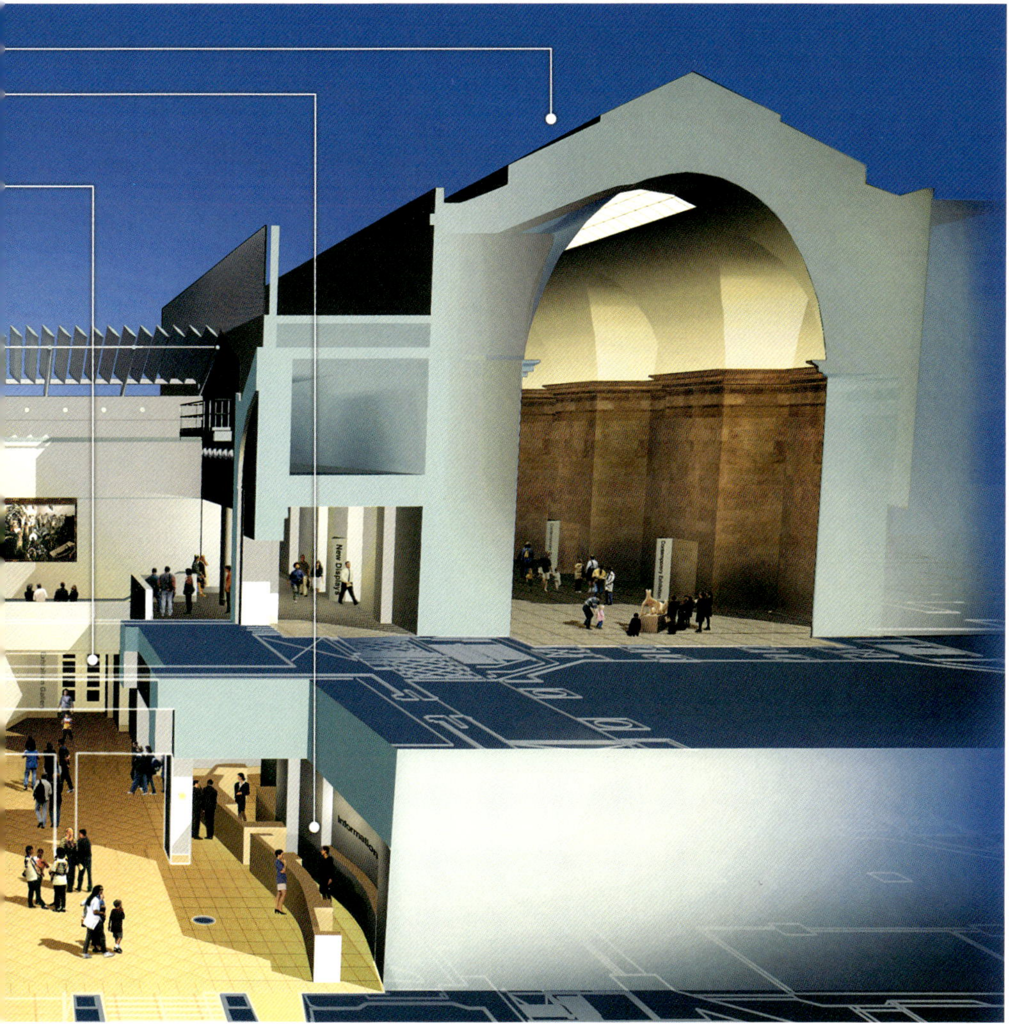
New Displays
Information

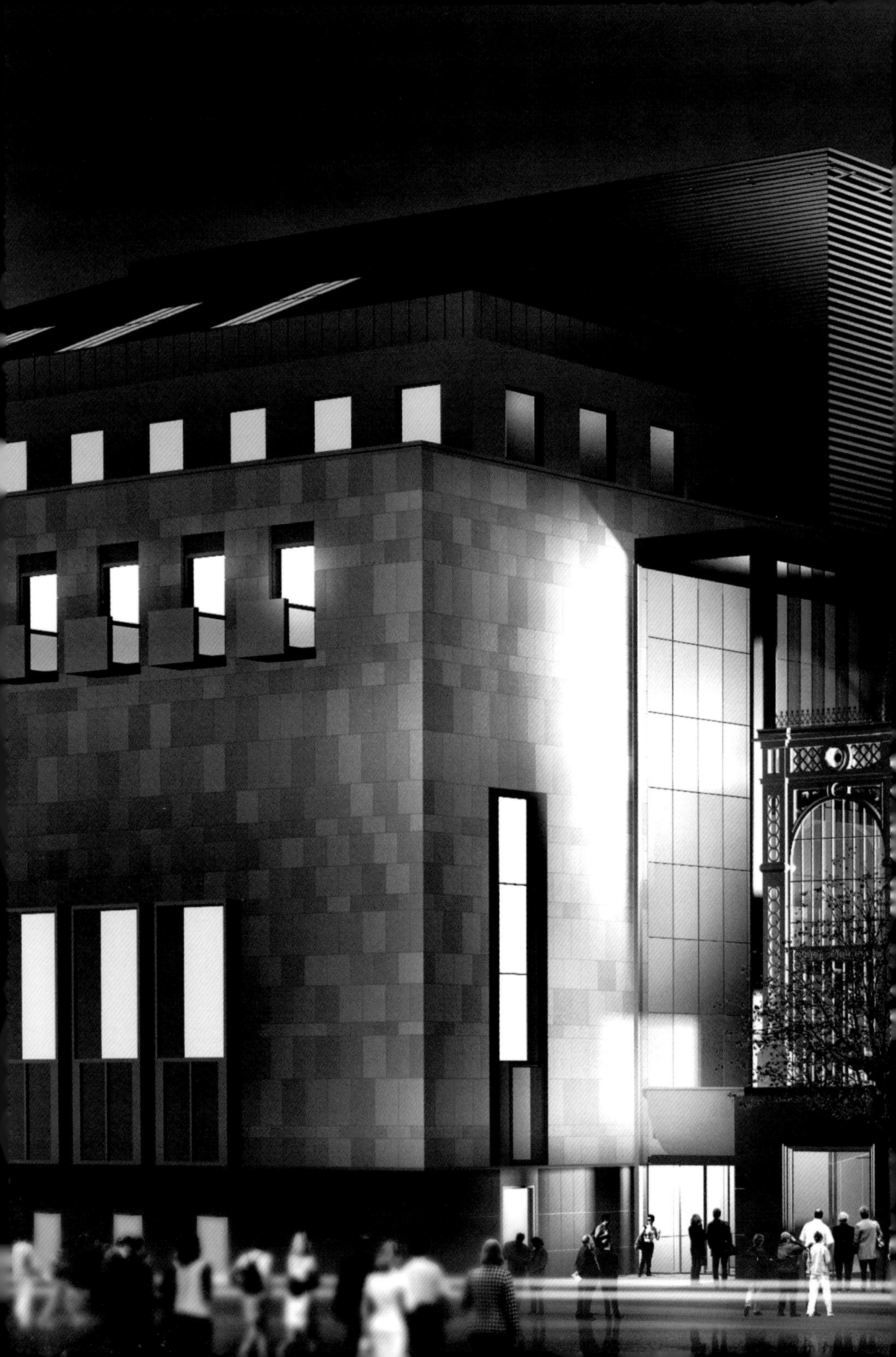

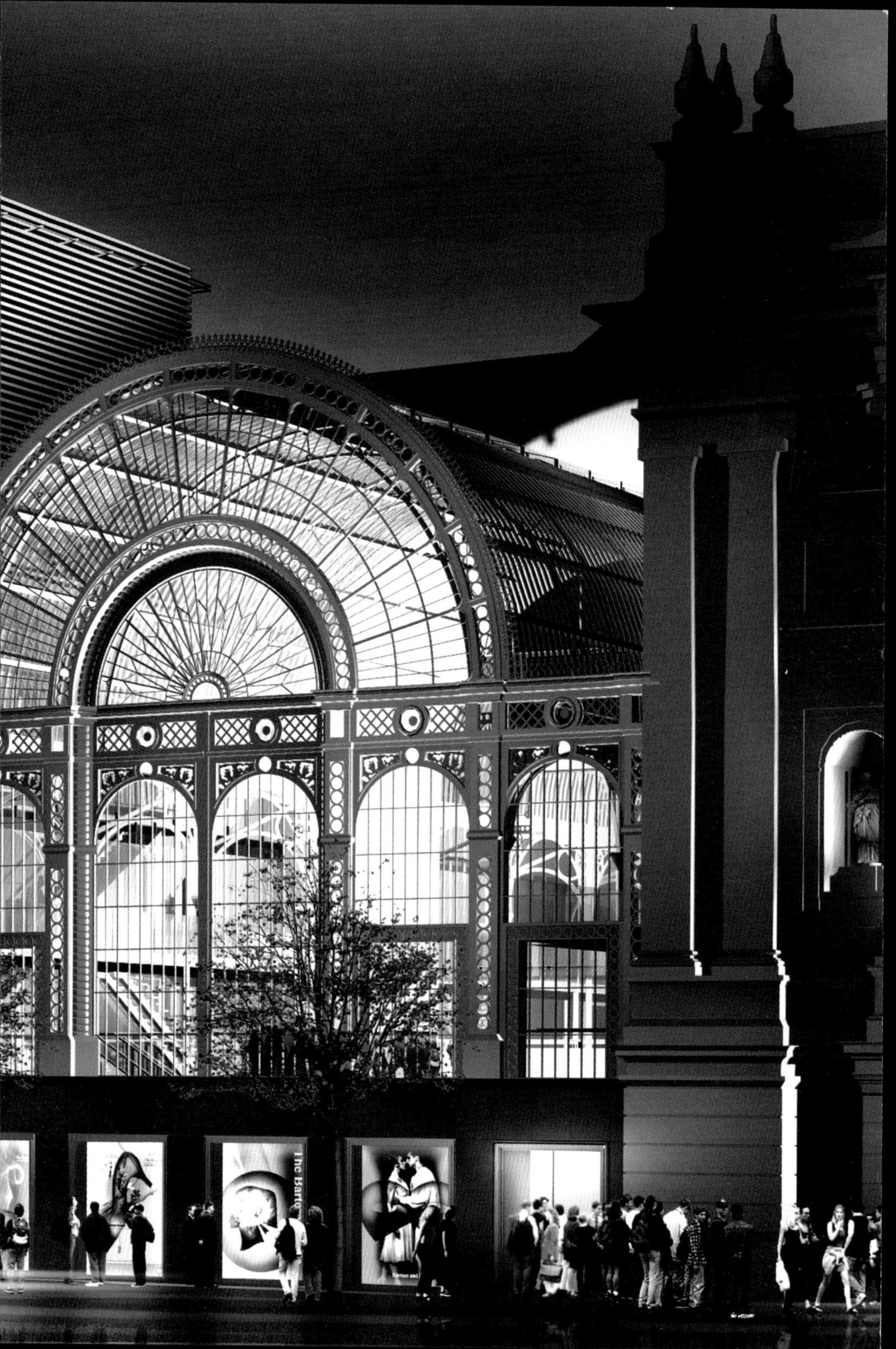

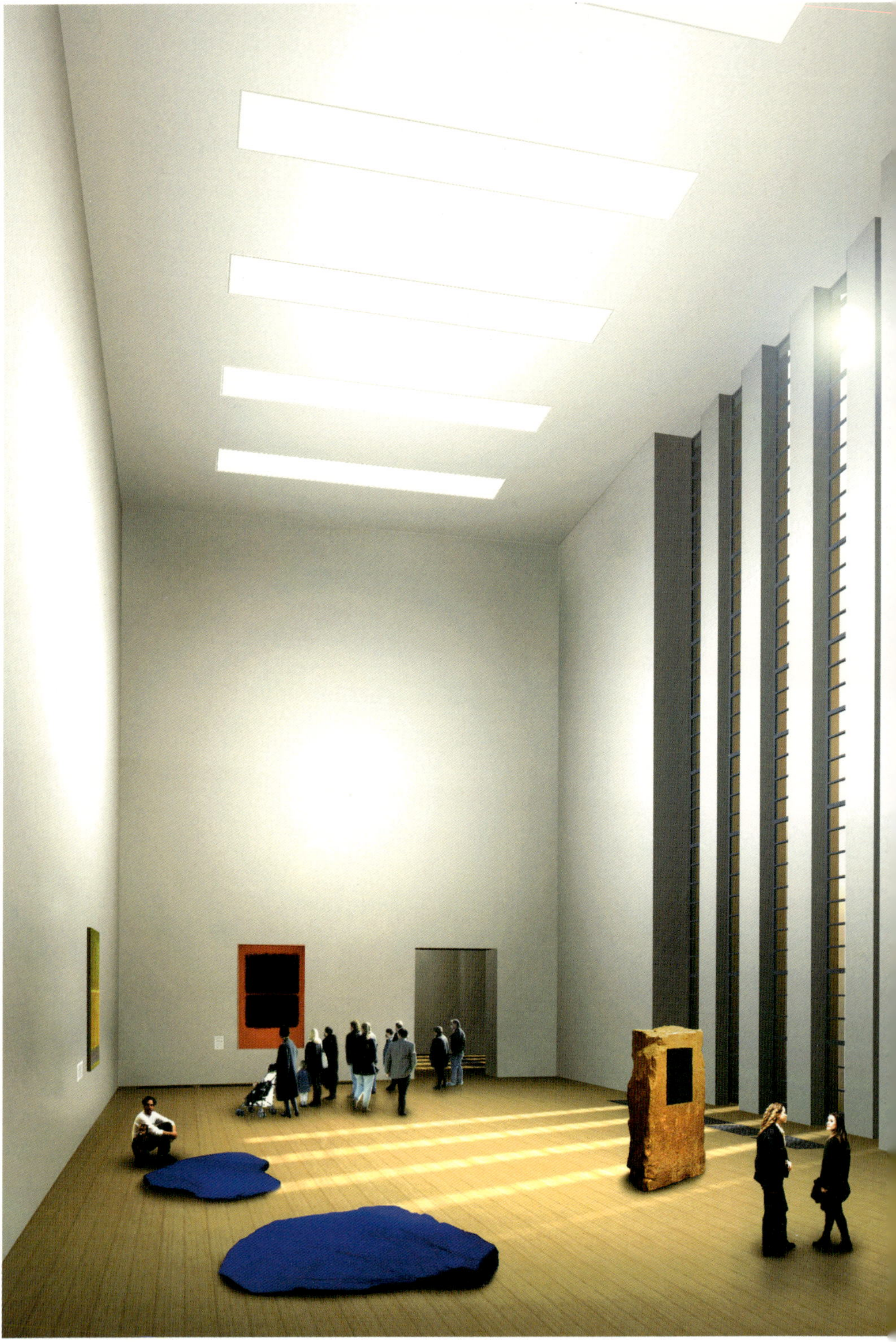

NPG 2000

The National Portrait Gallery's Millennium Development Project

Opens May 2000

1. The Rooftop Restaurant
2. The Tudor Gallery
3. The Balcony Gallery
4. Entrance Hall, leading to The IT Gallery
5. Lecture Theatre
6. Existing galleries

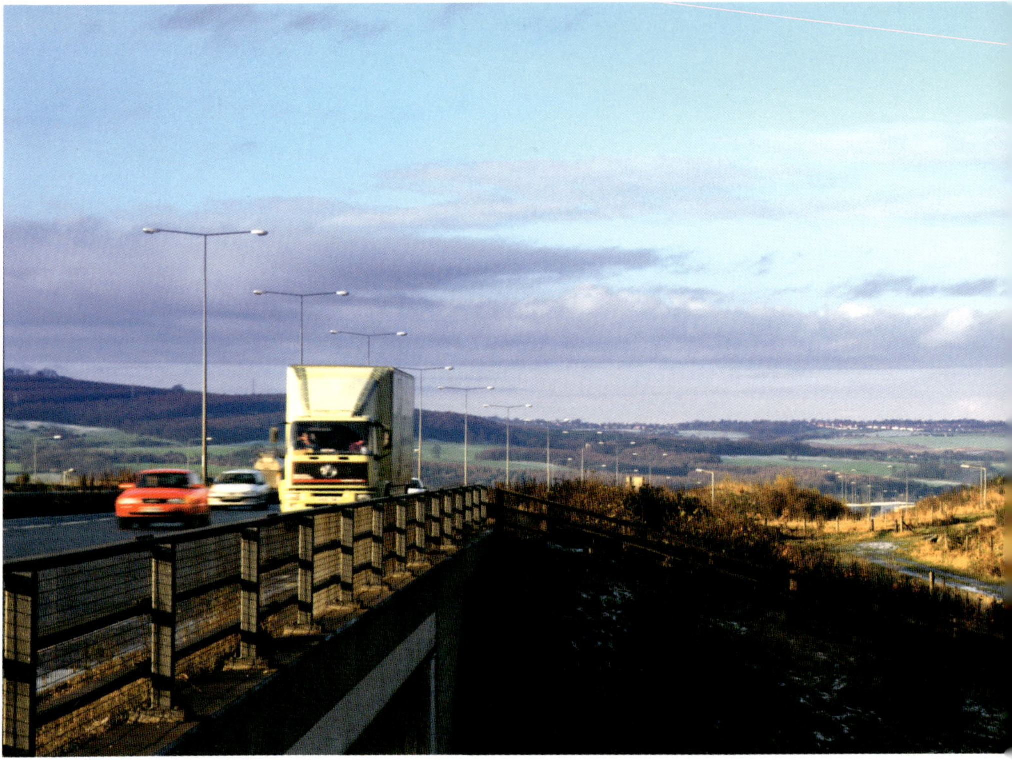

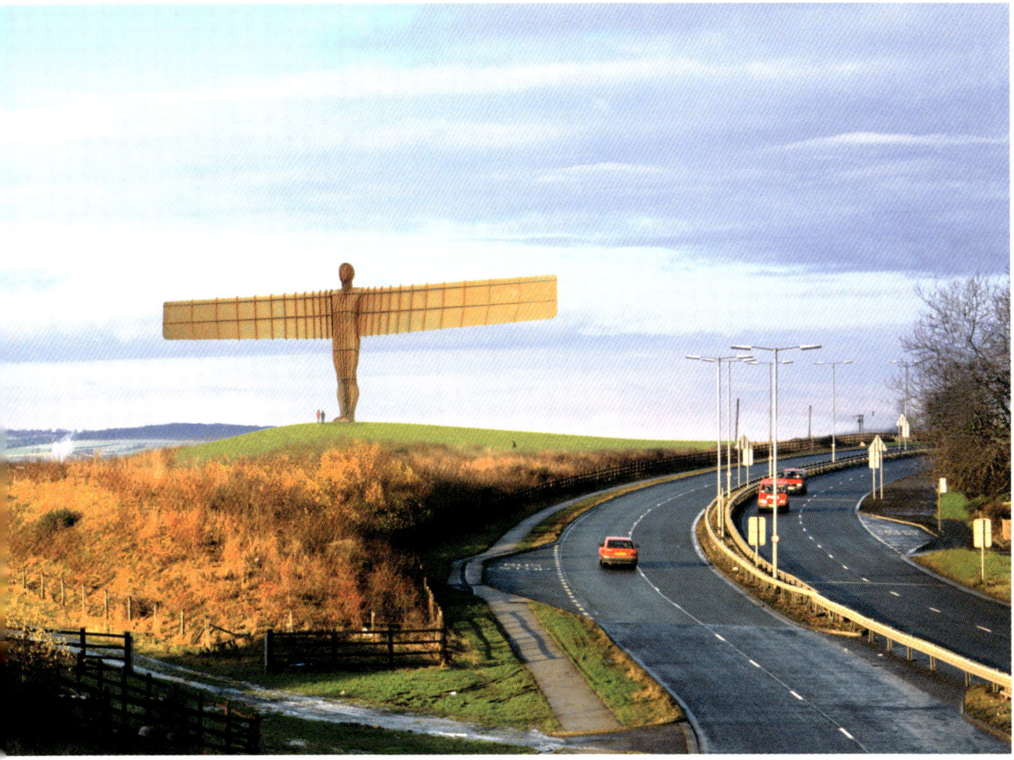

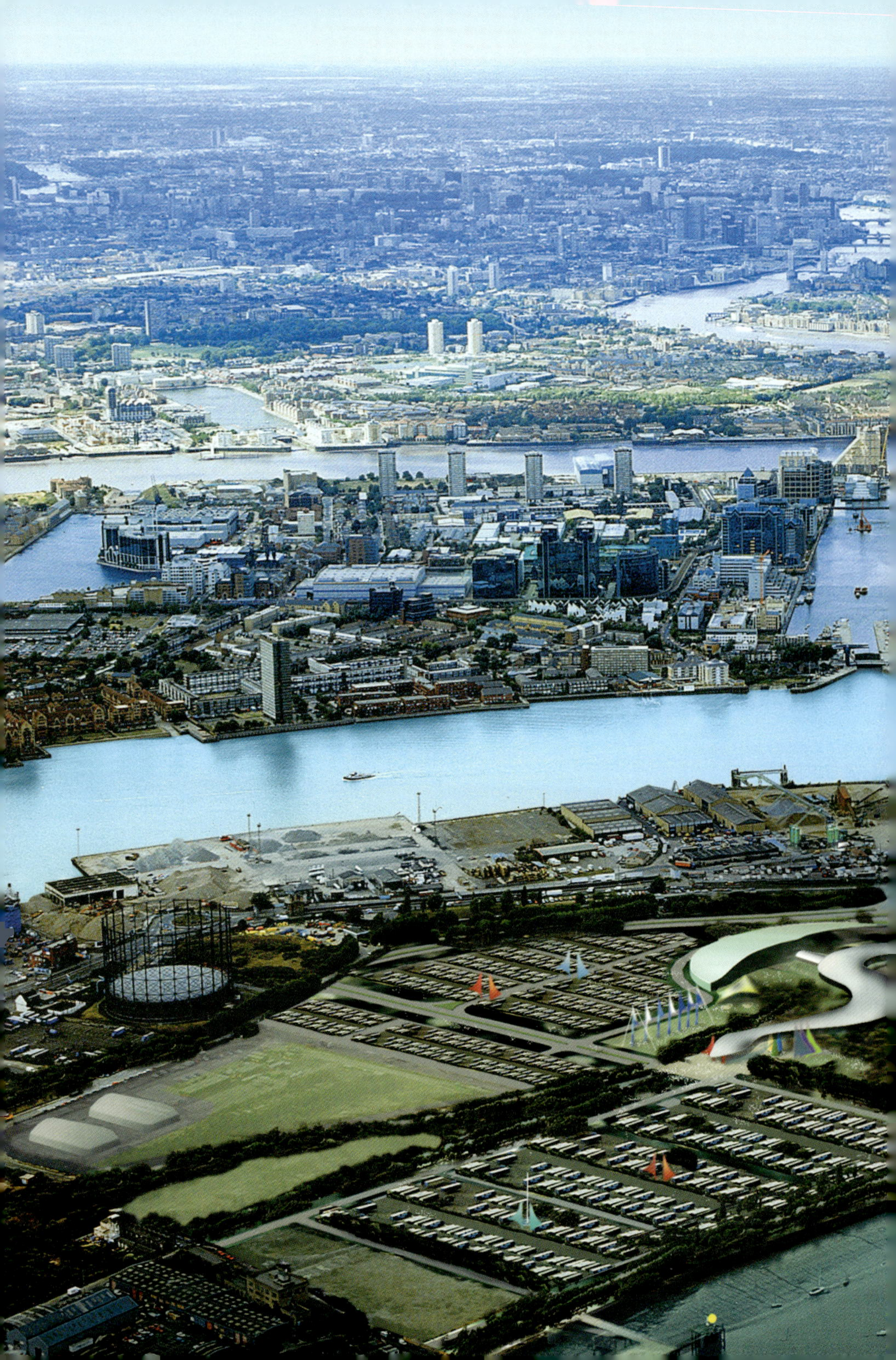

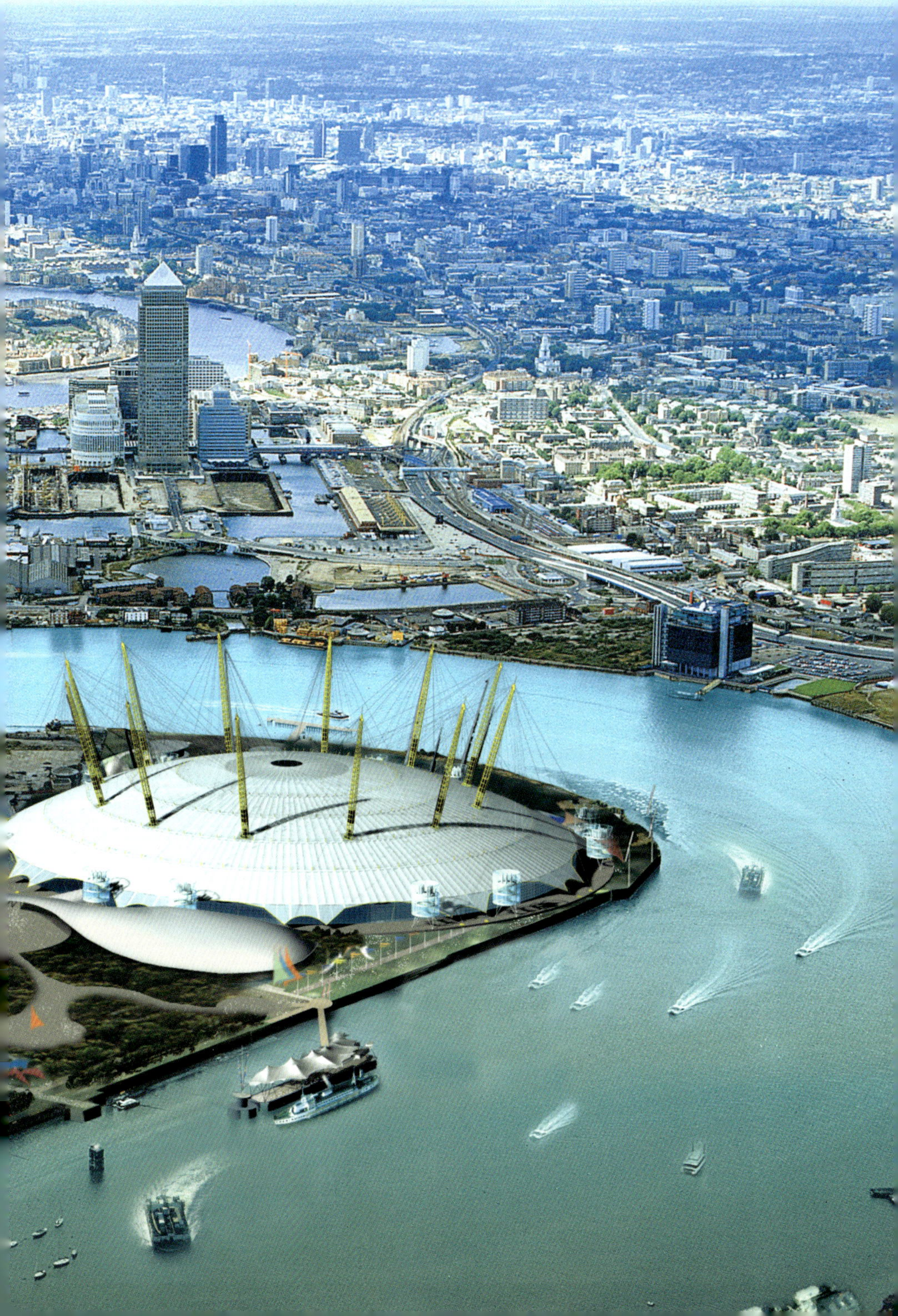

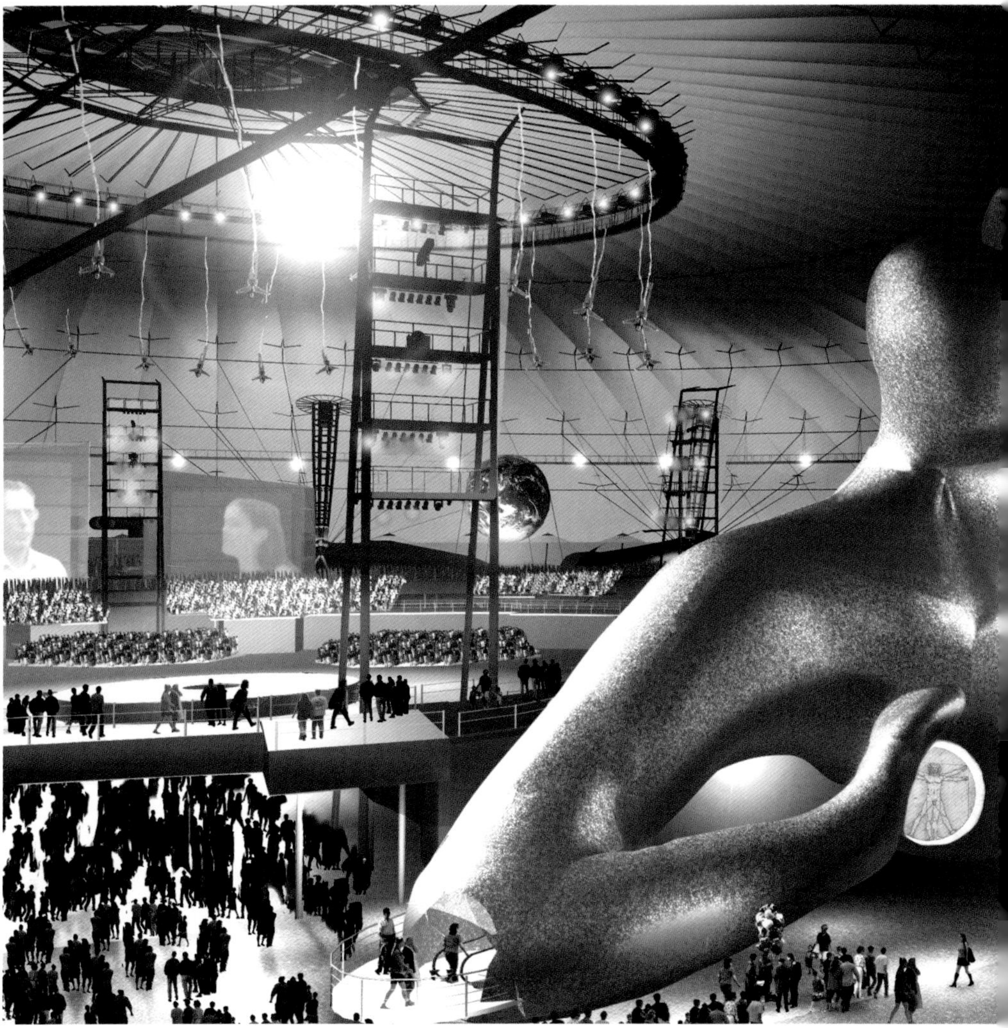

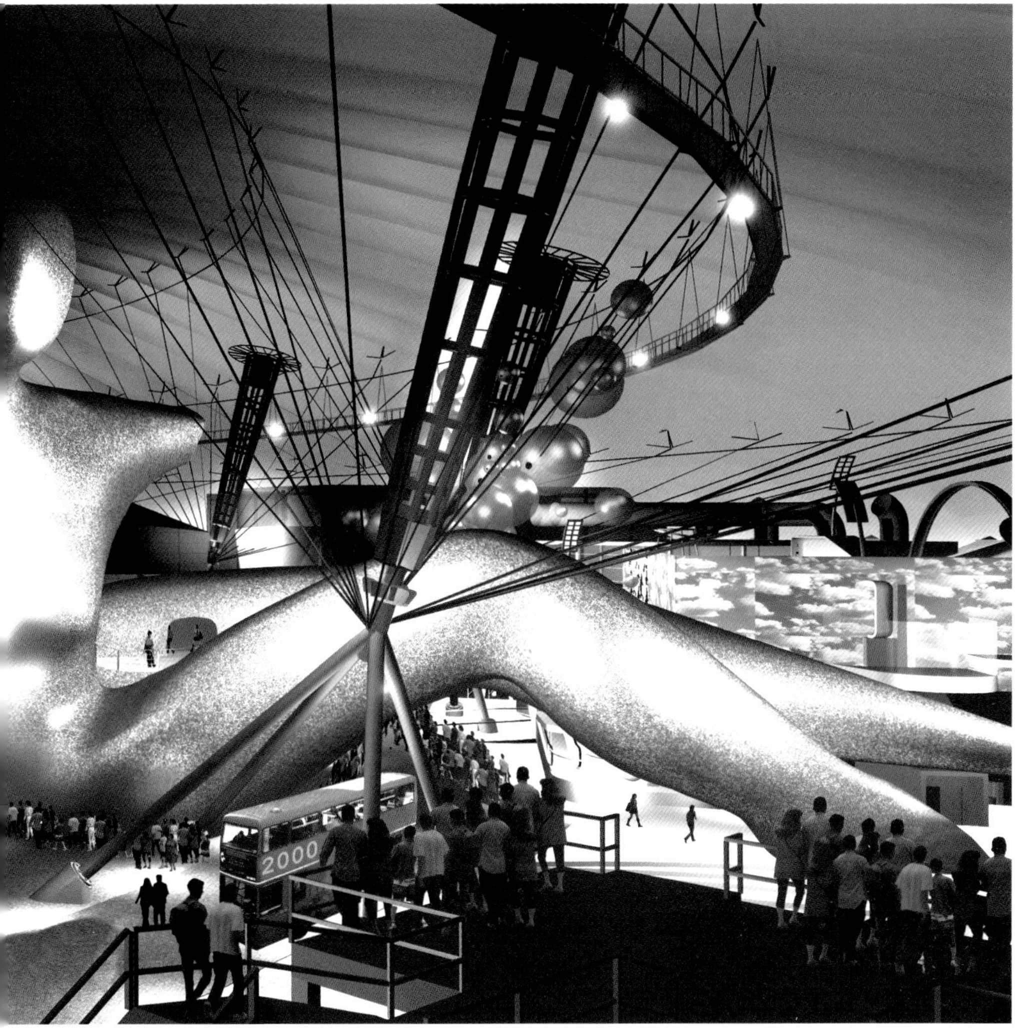
2000

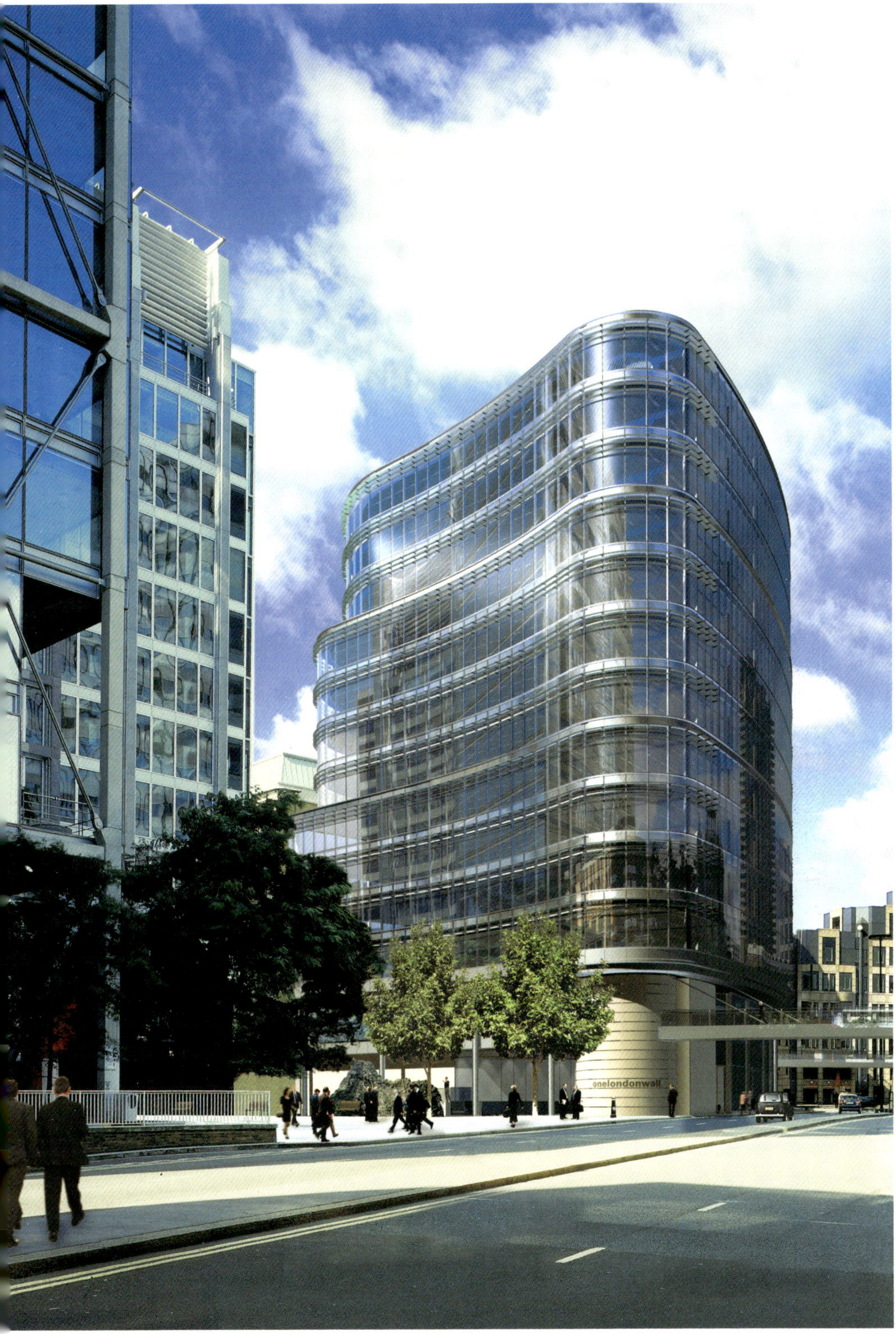
onelondonwall

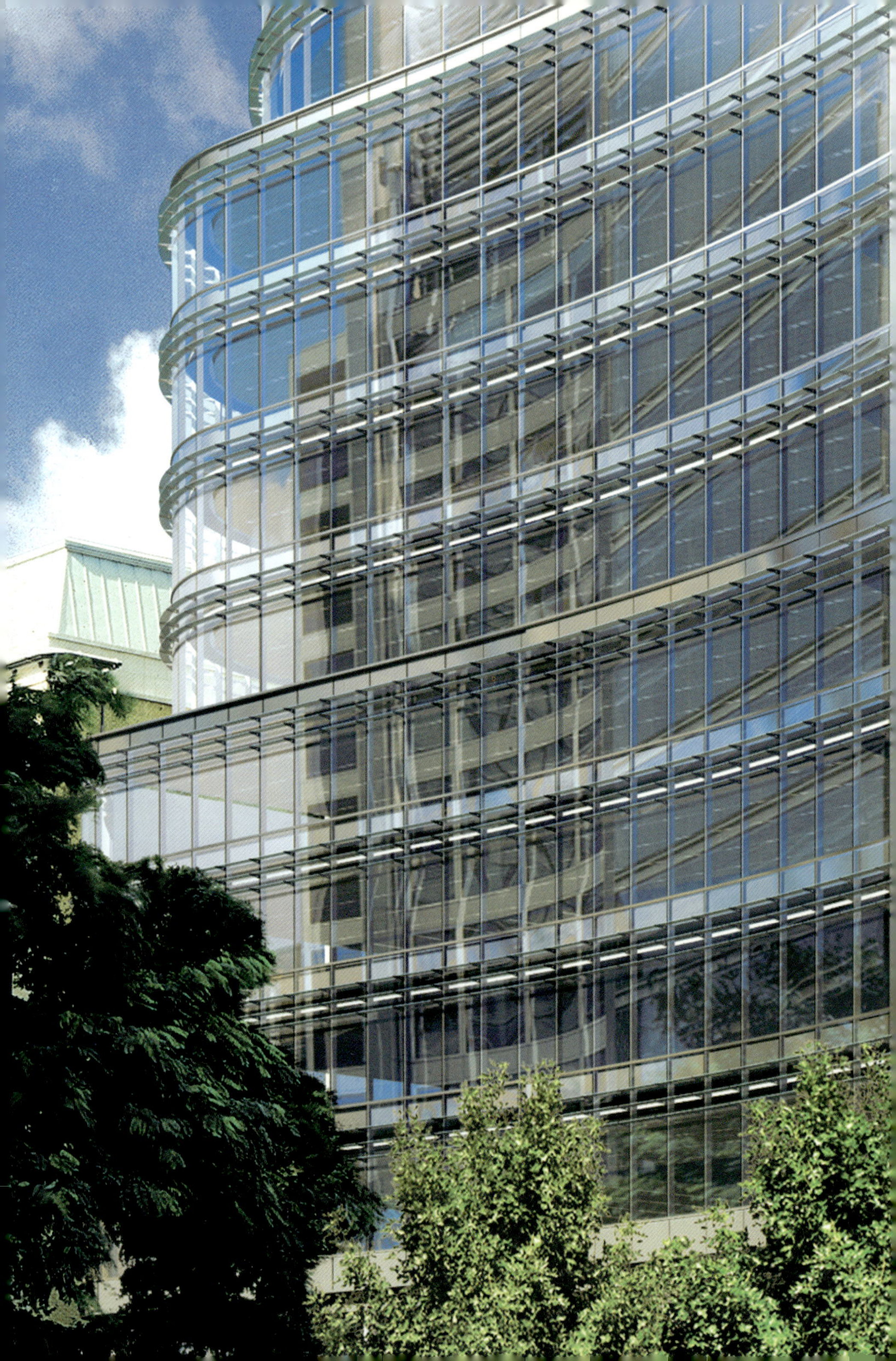

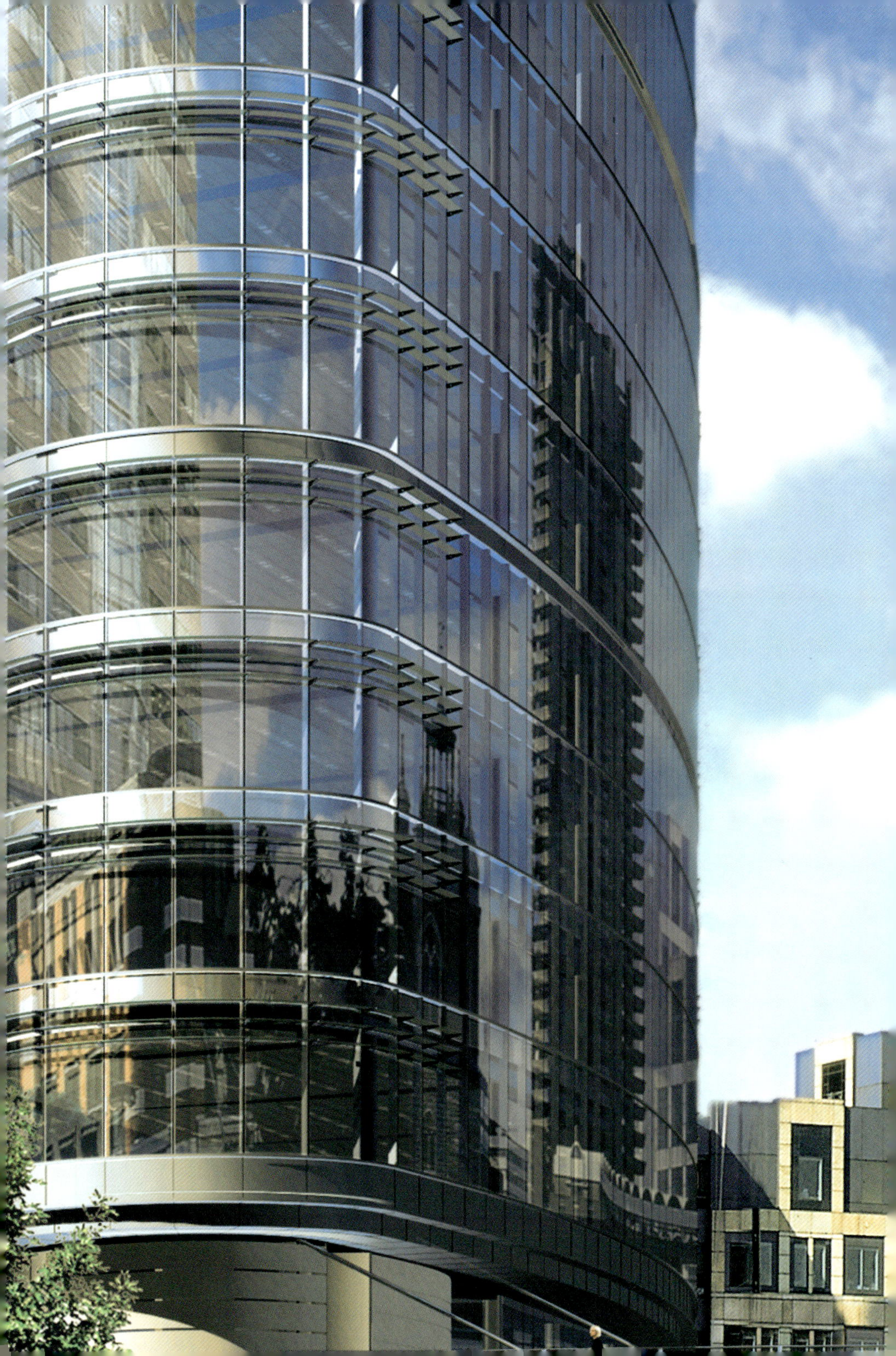

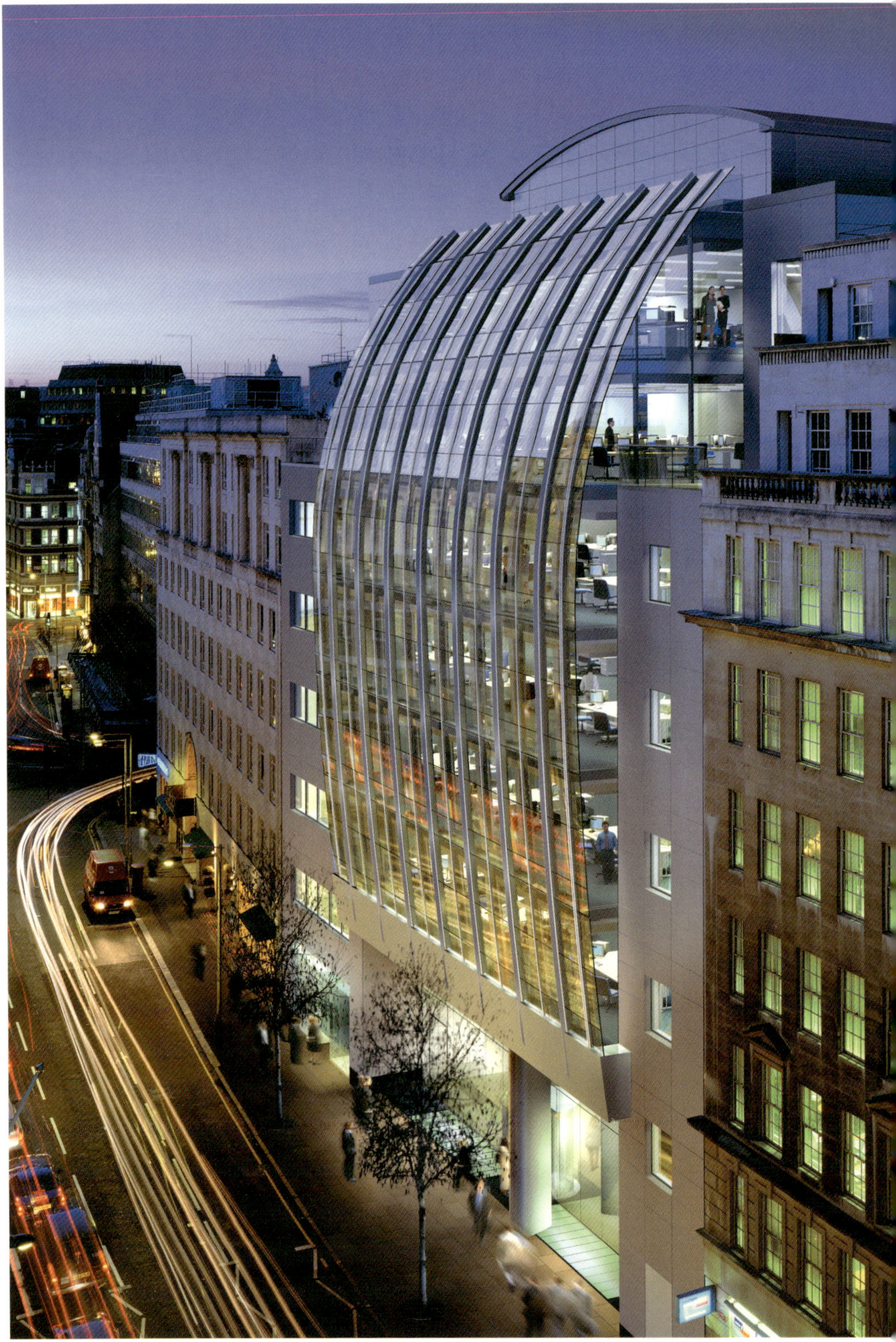

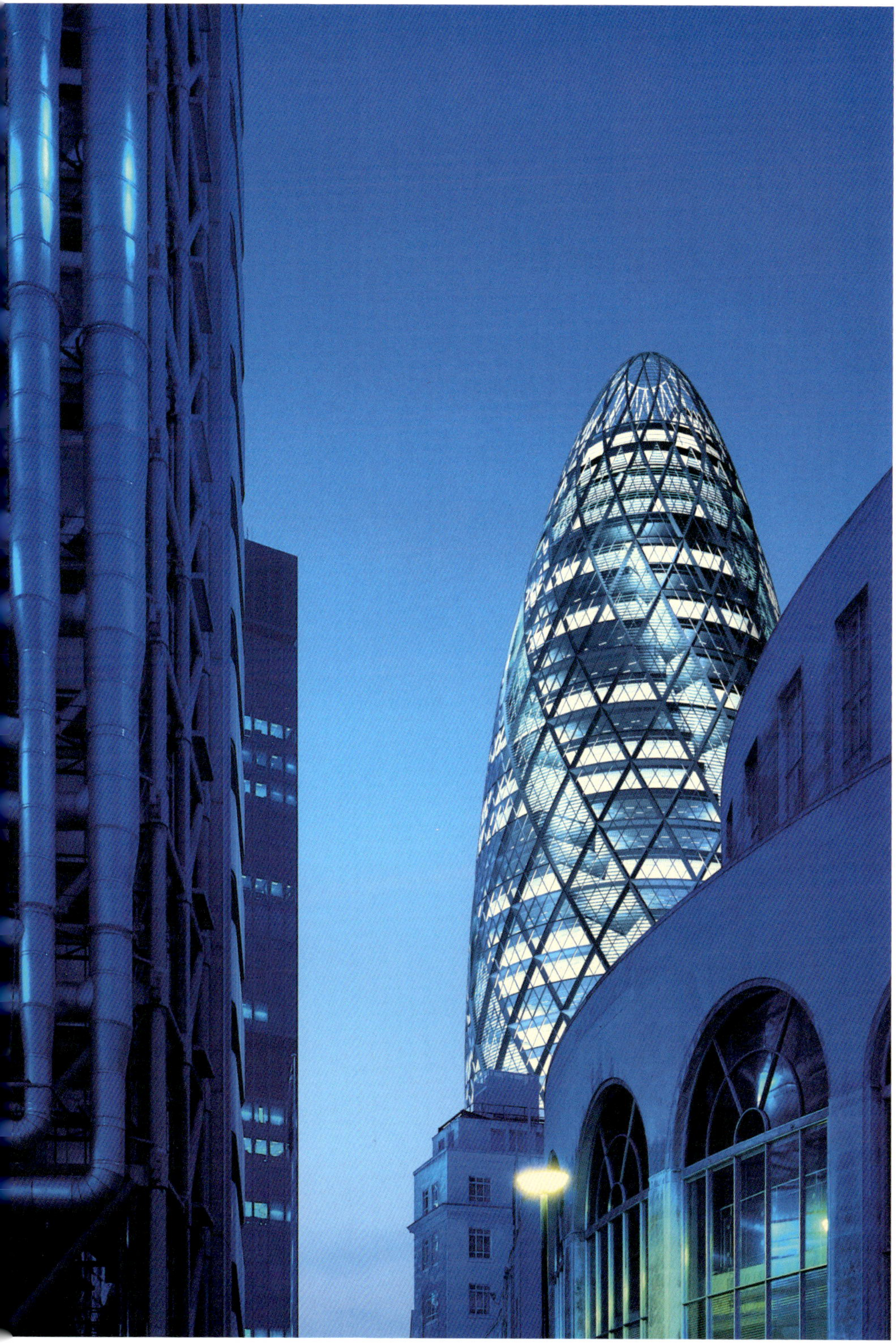

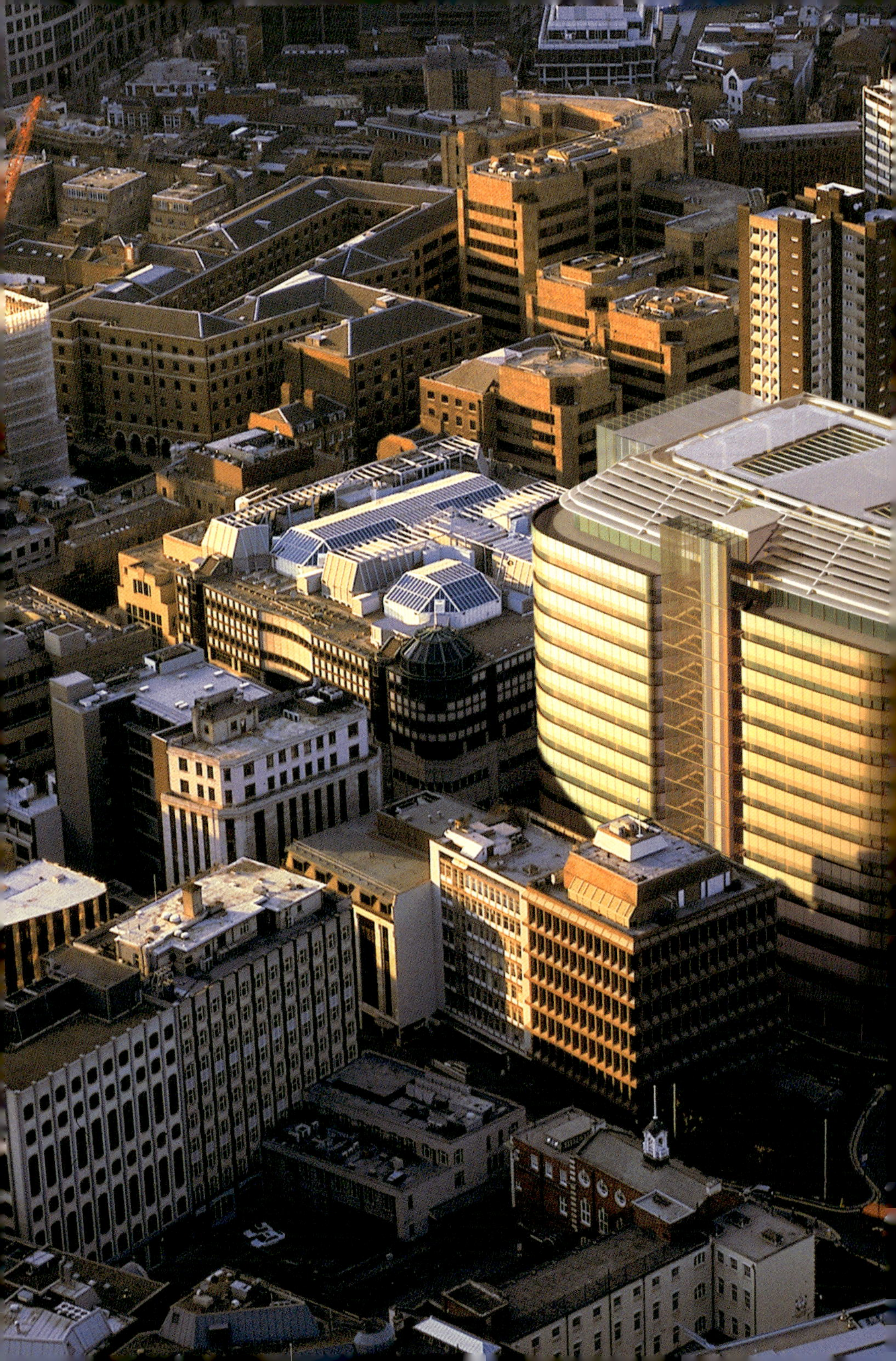

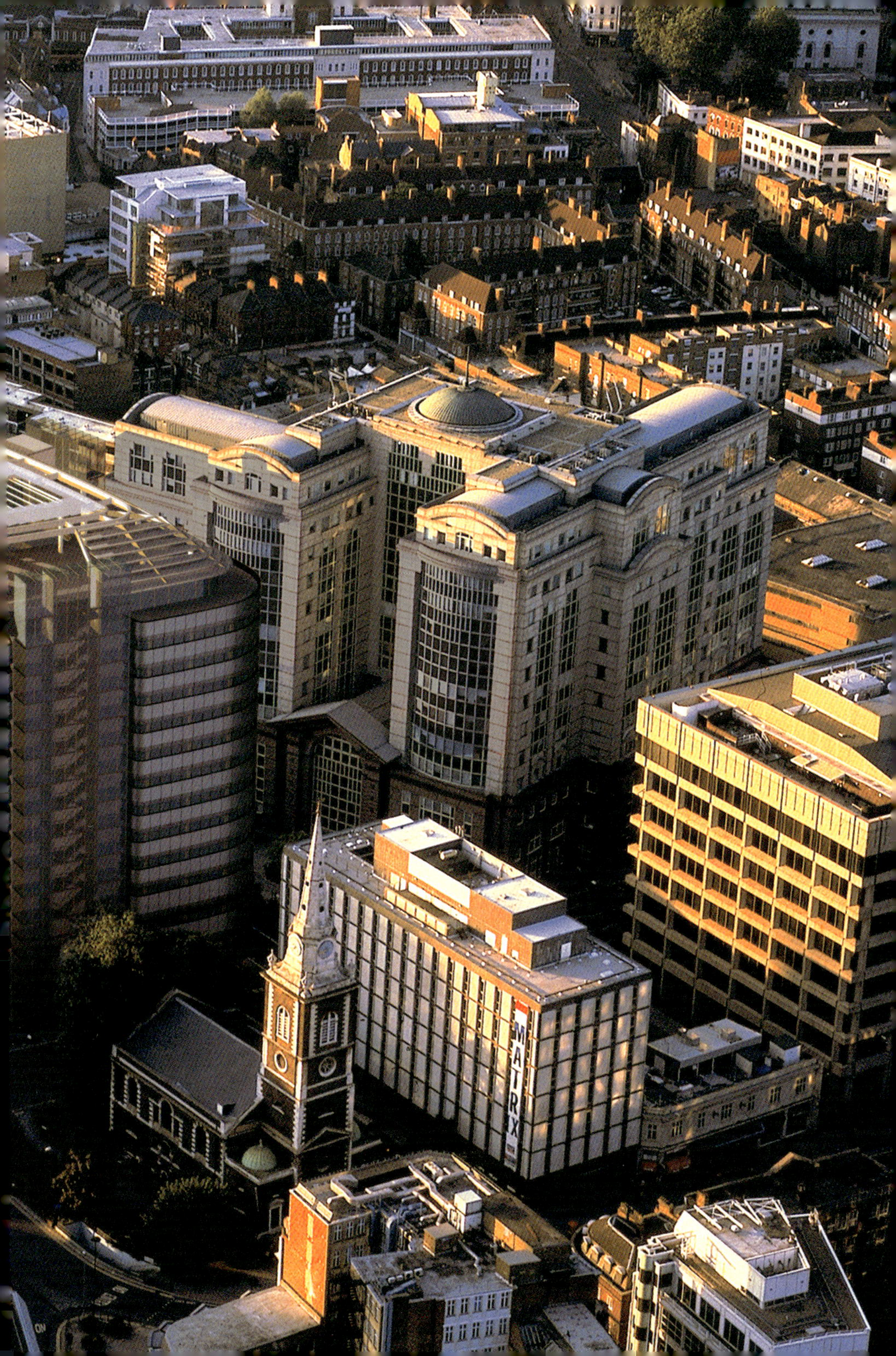
MATRX

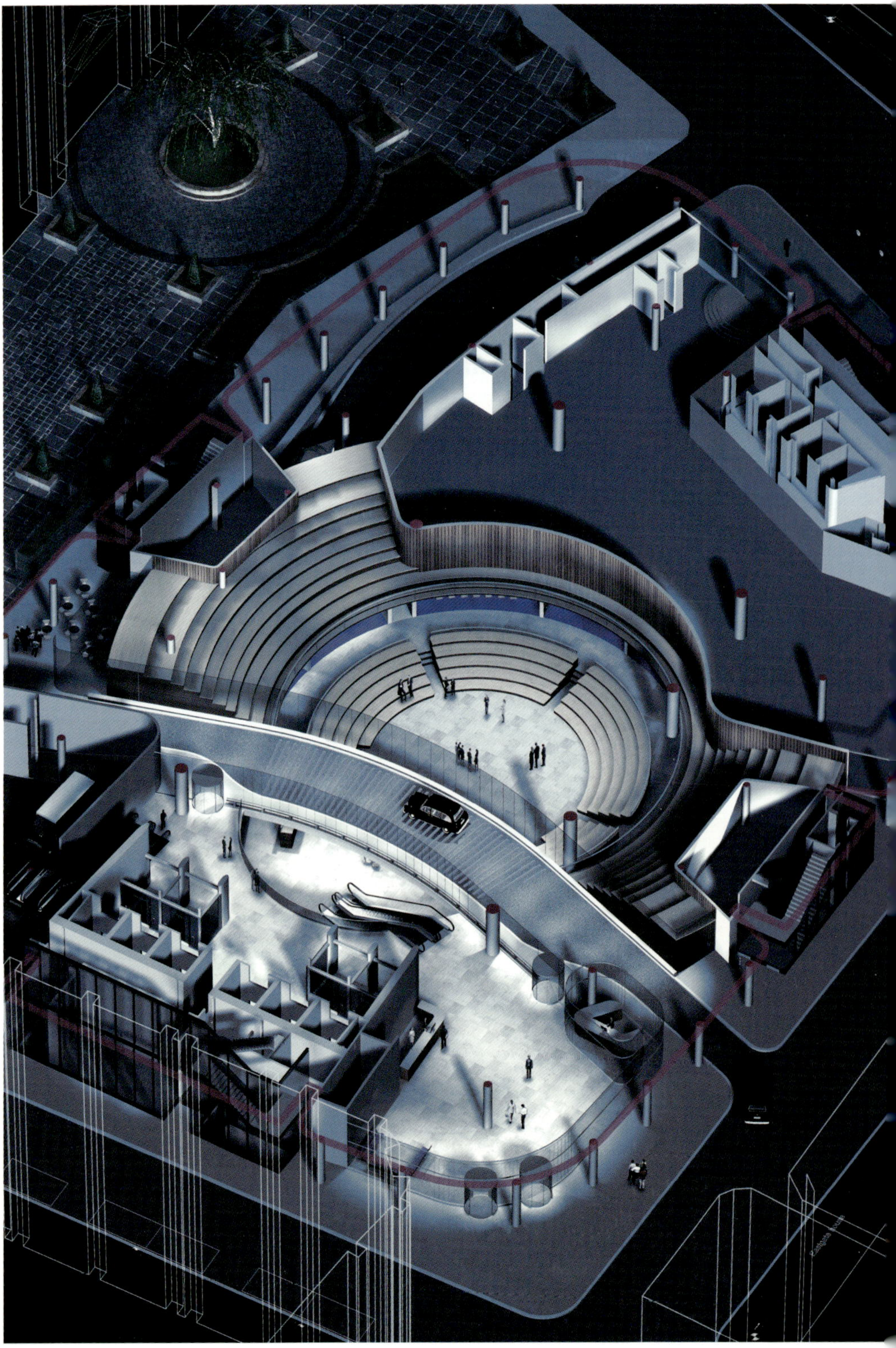

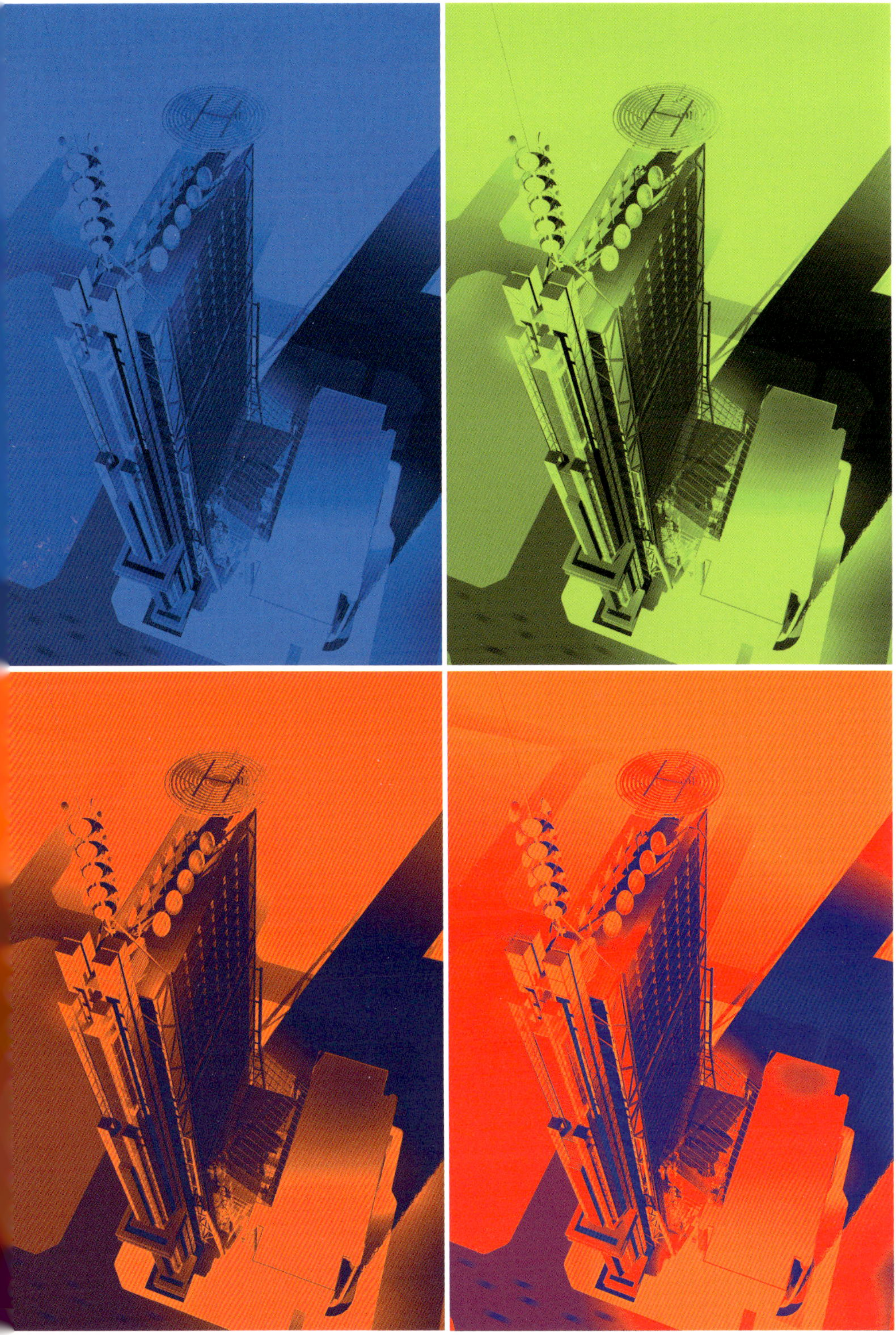

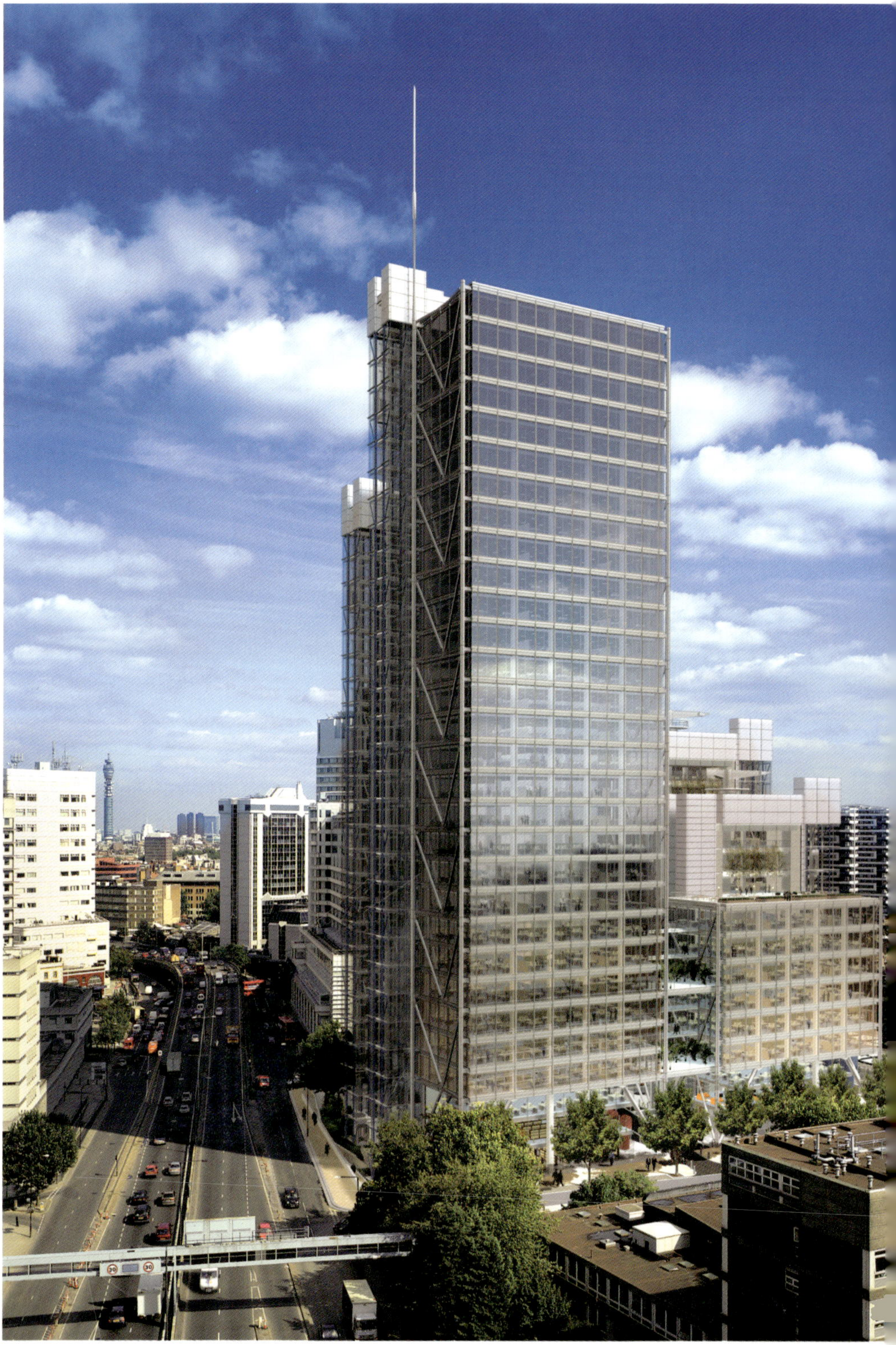

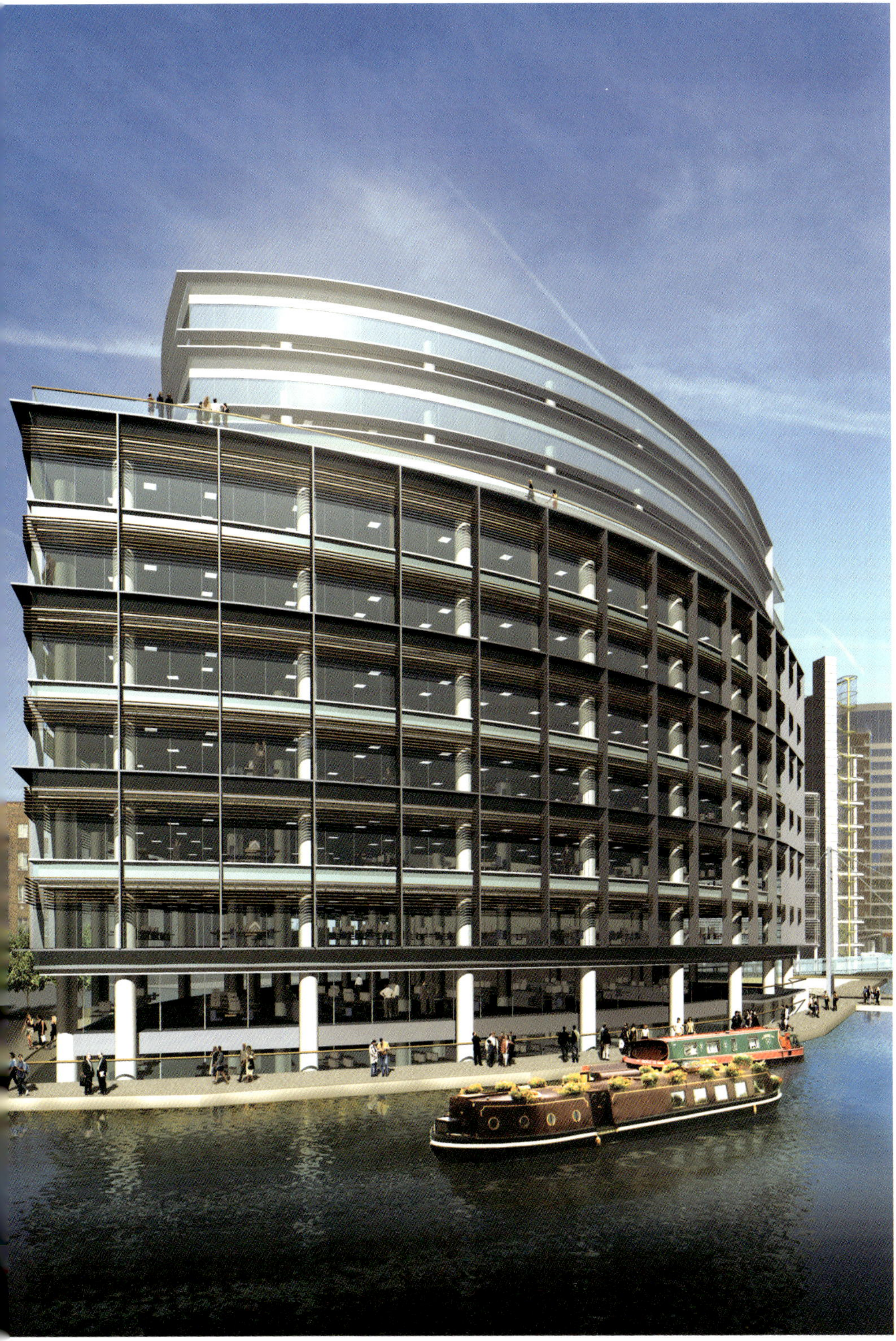

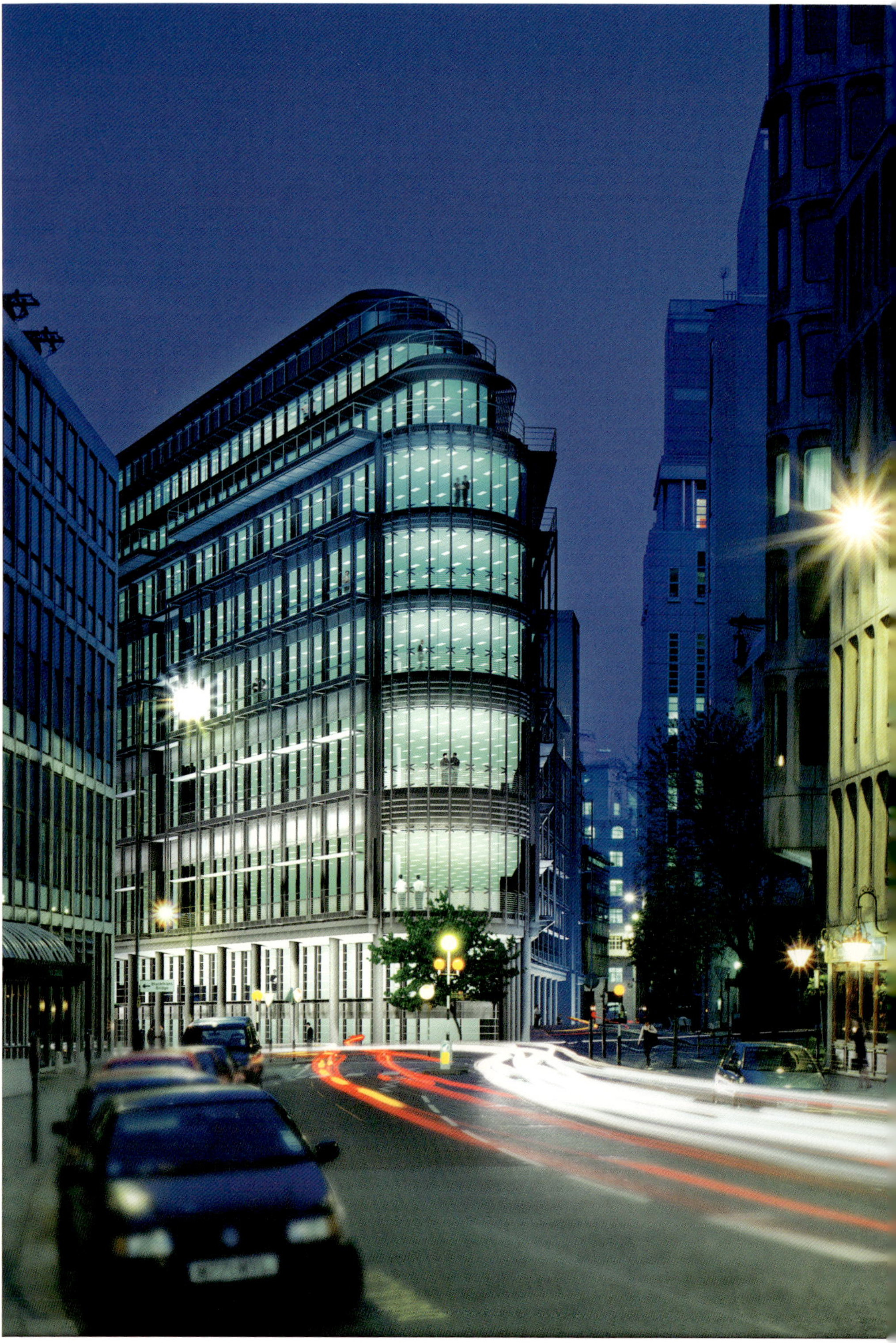

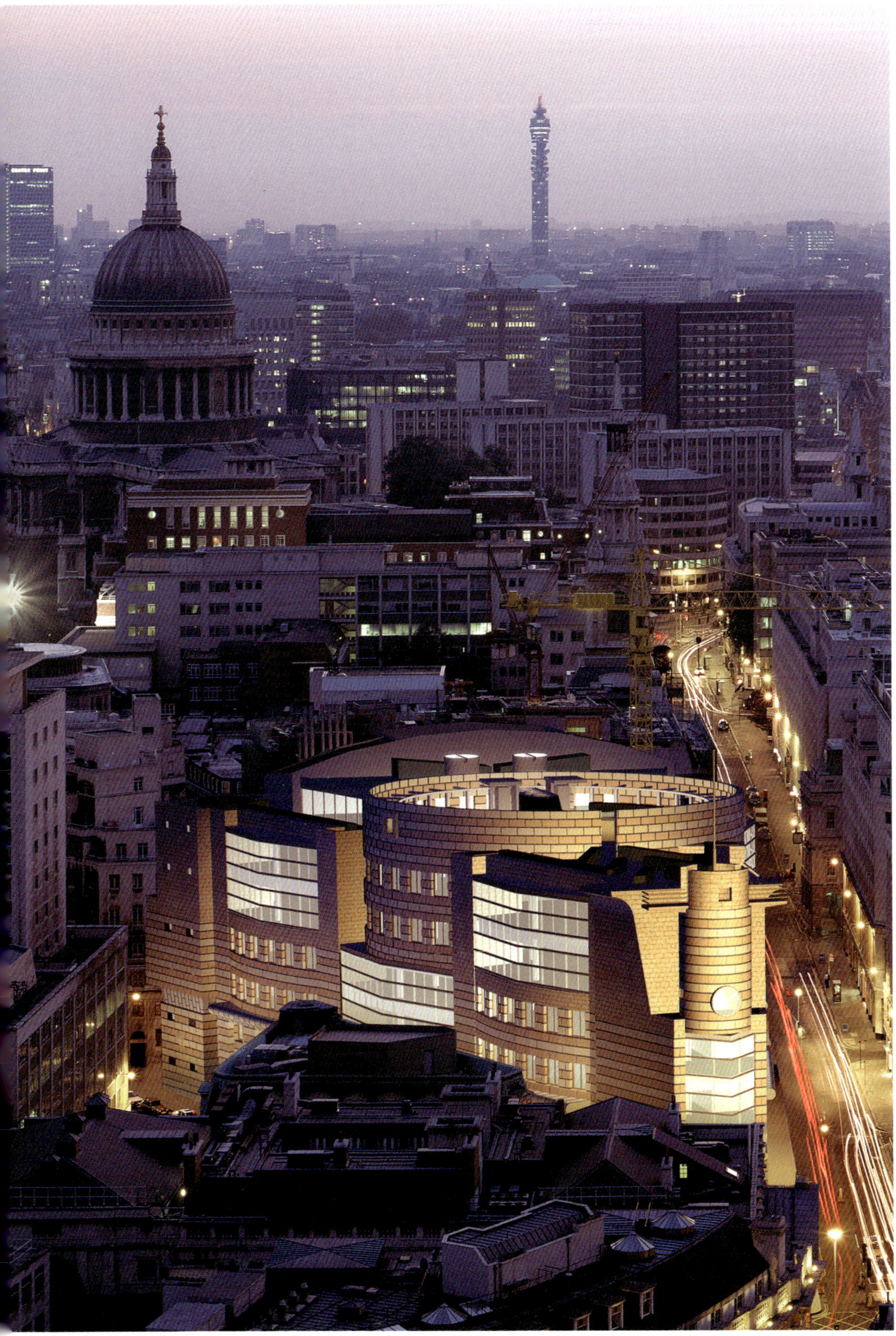

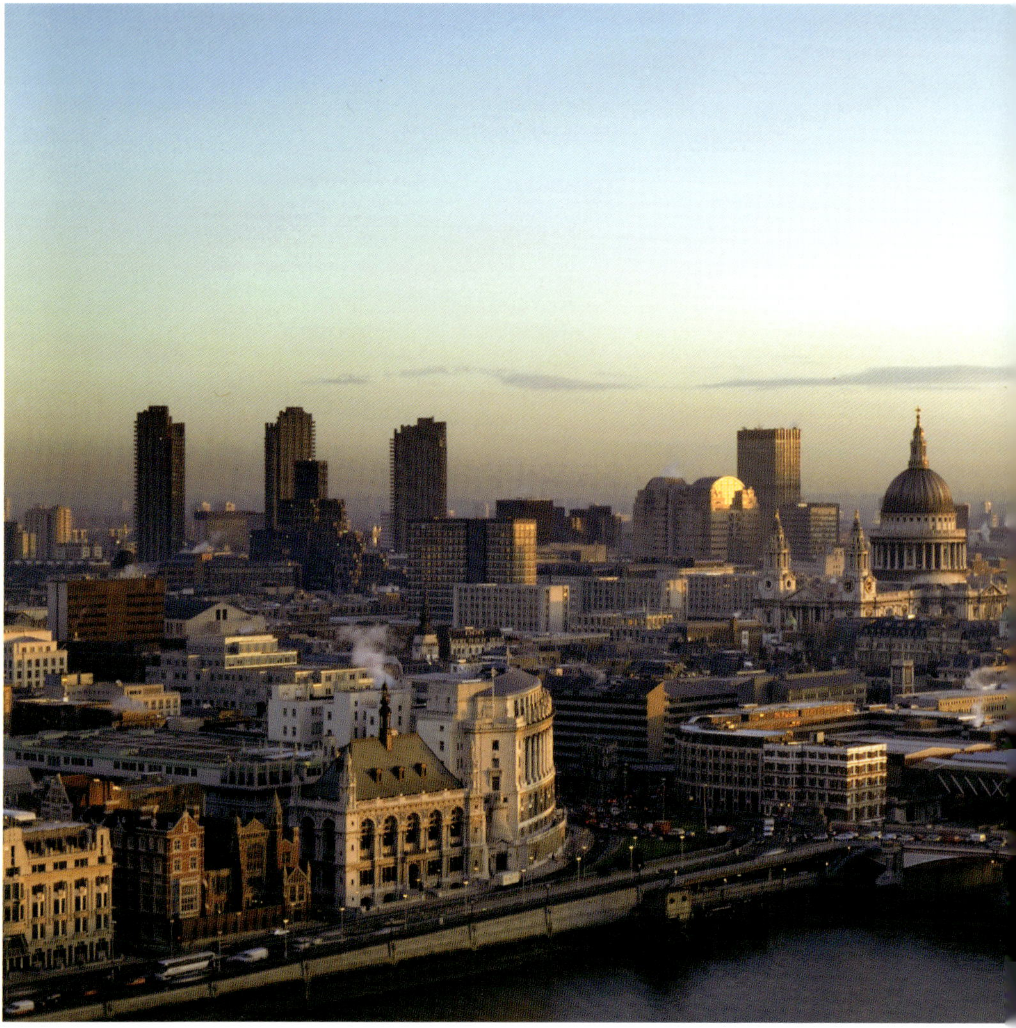

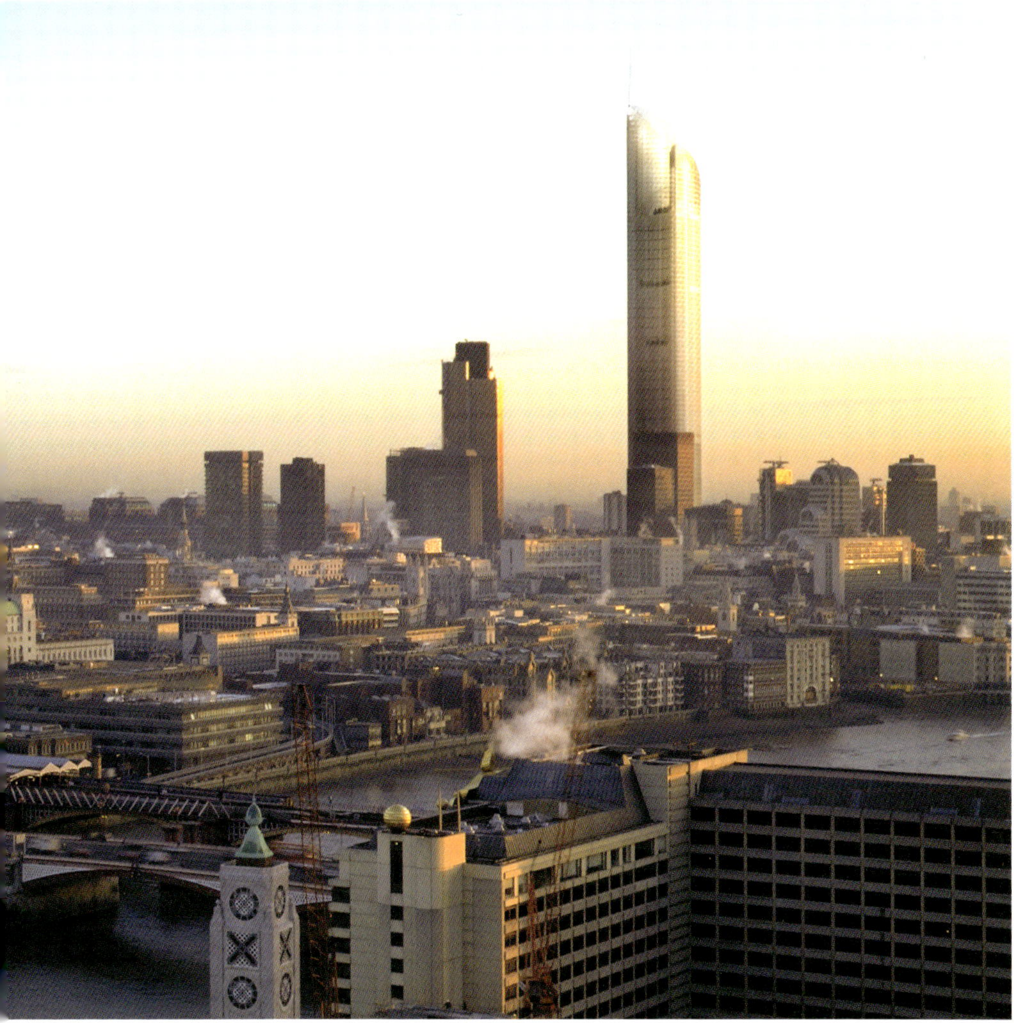

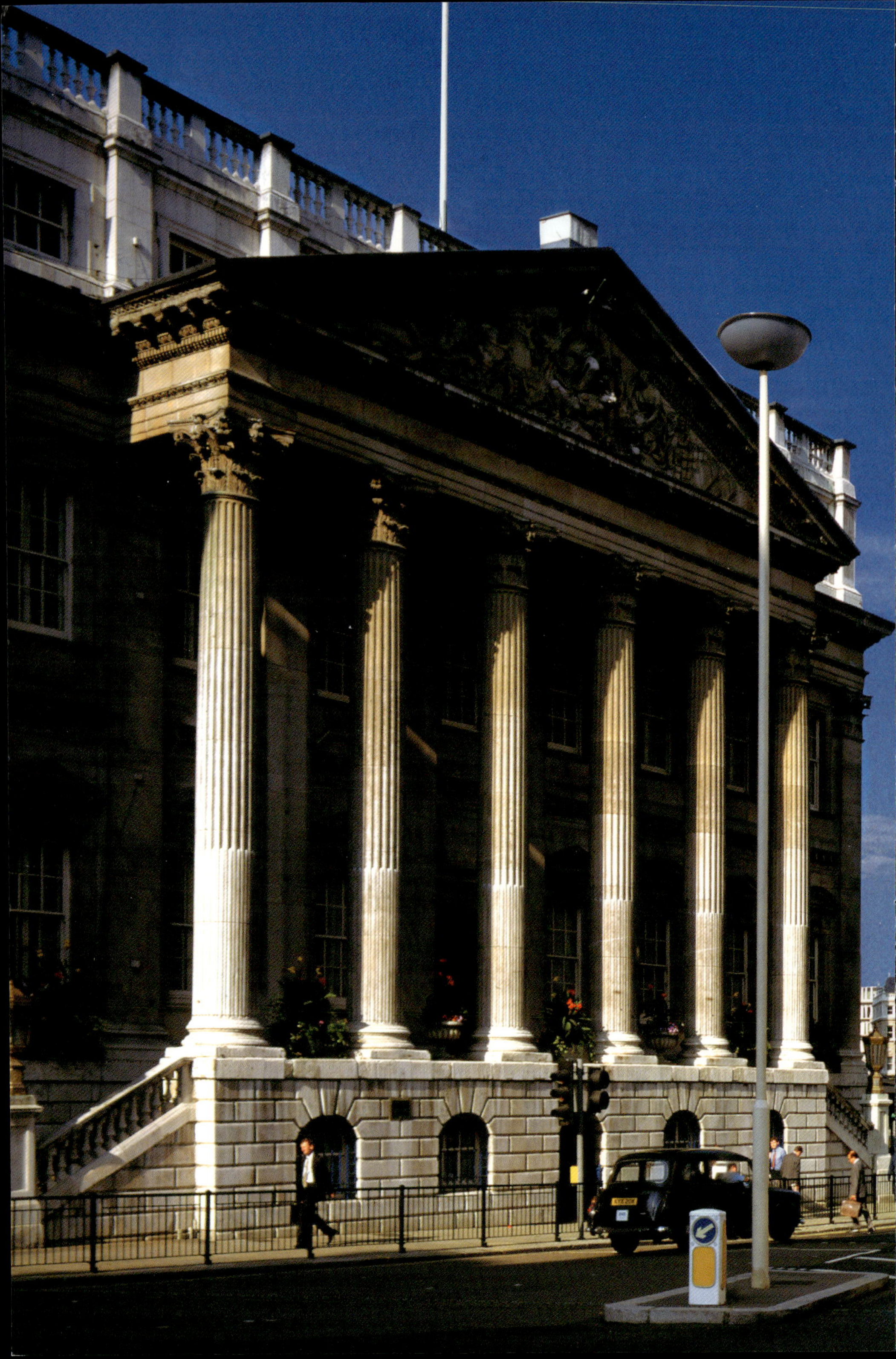

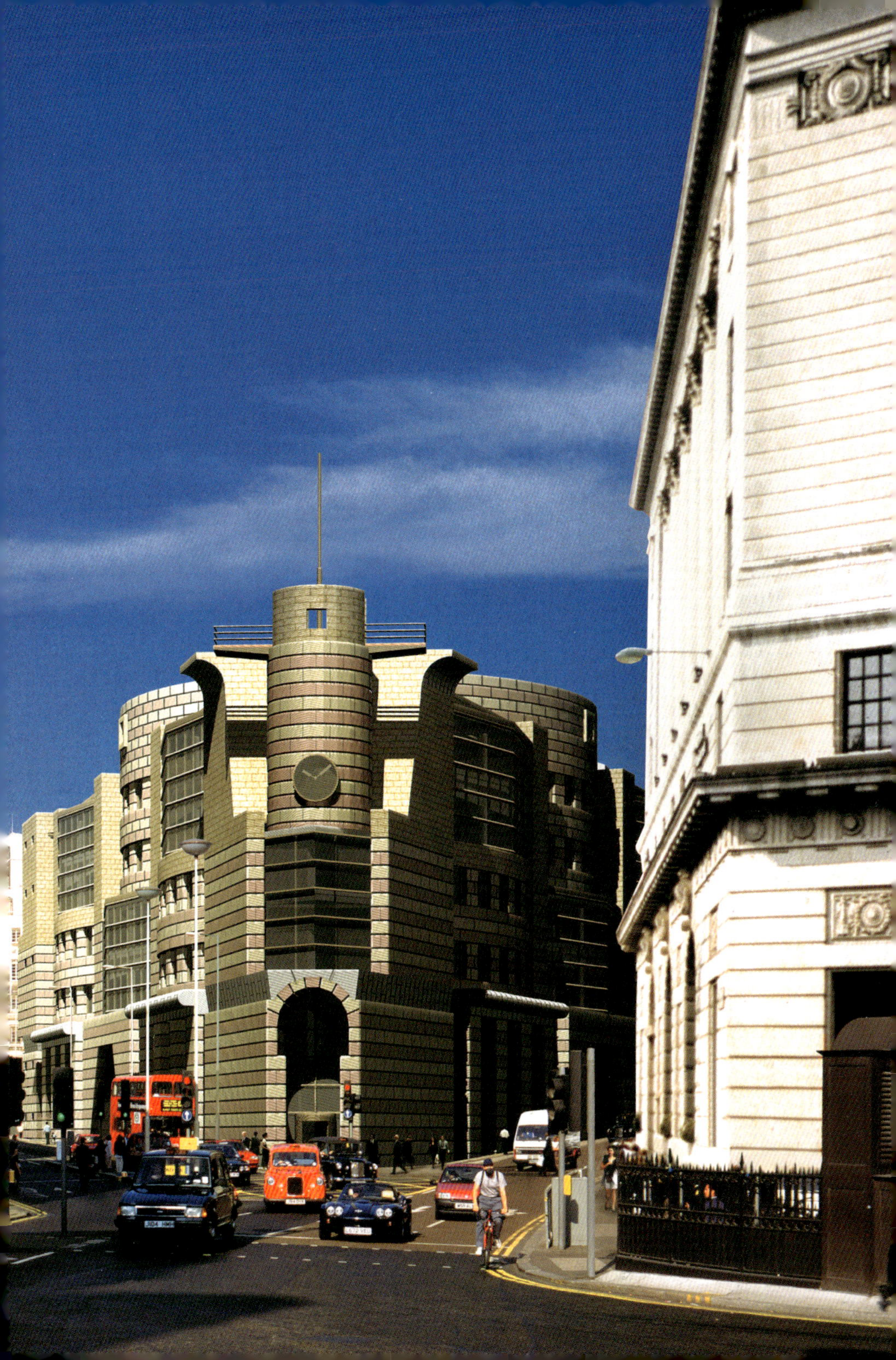

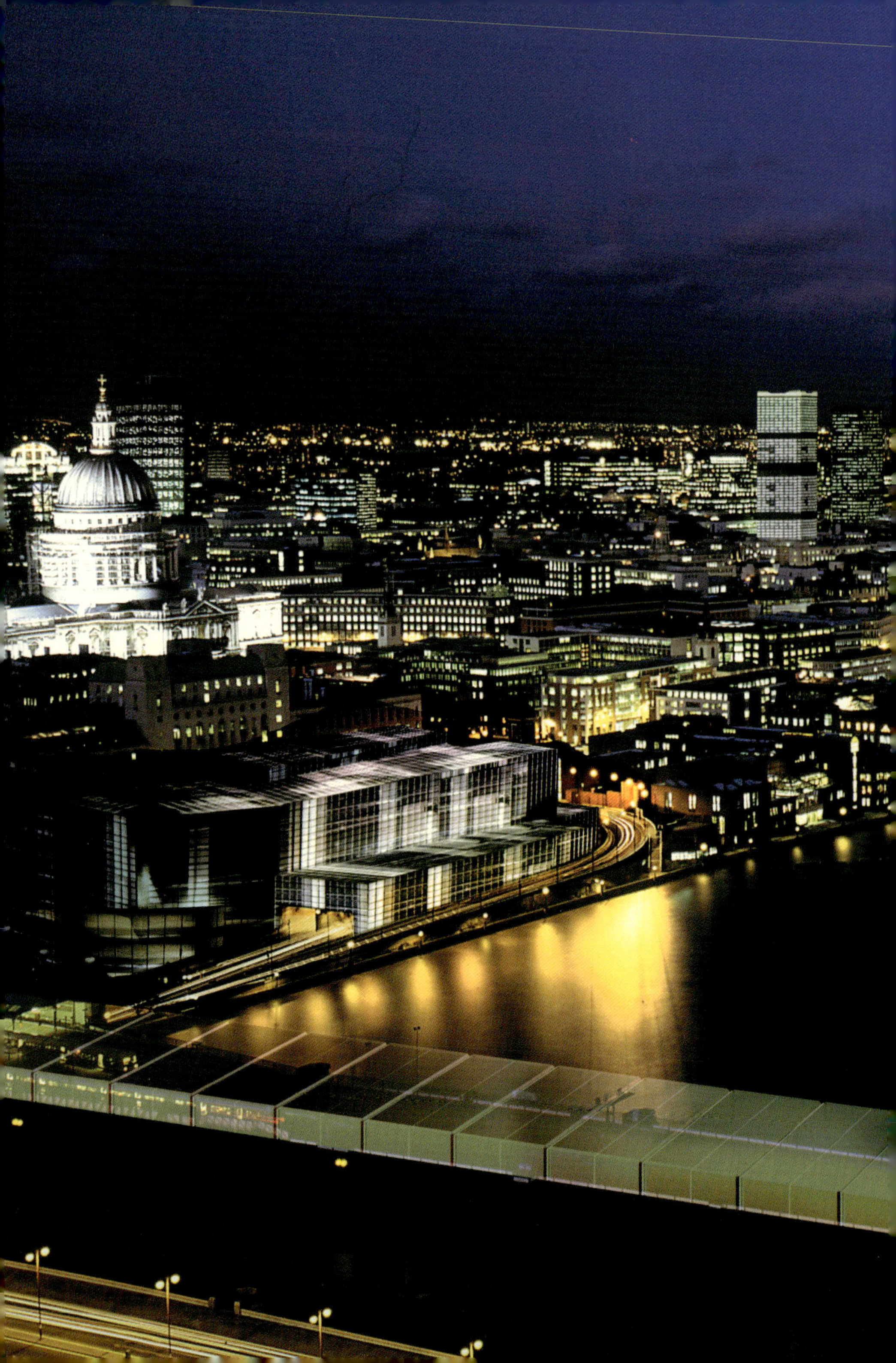

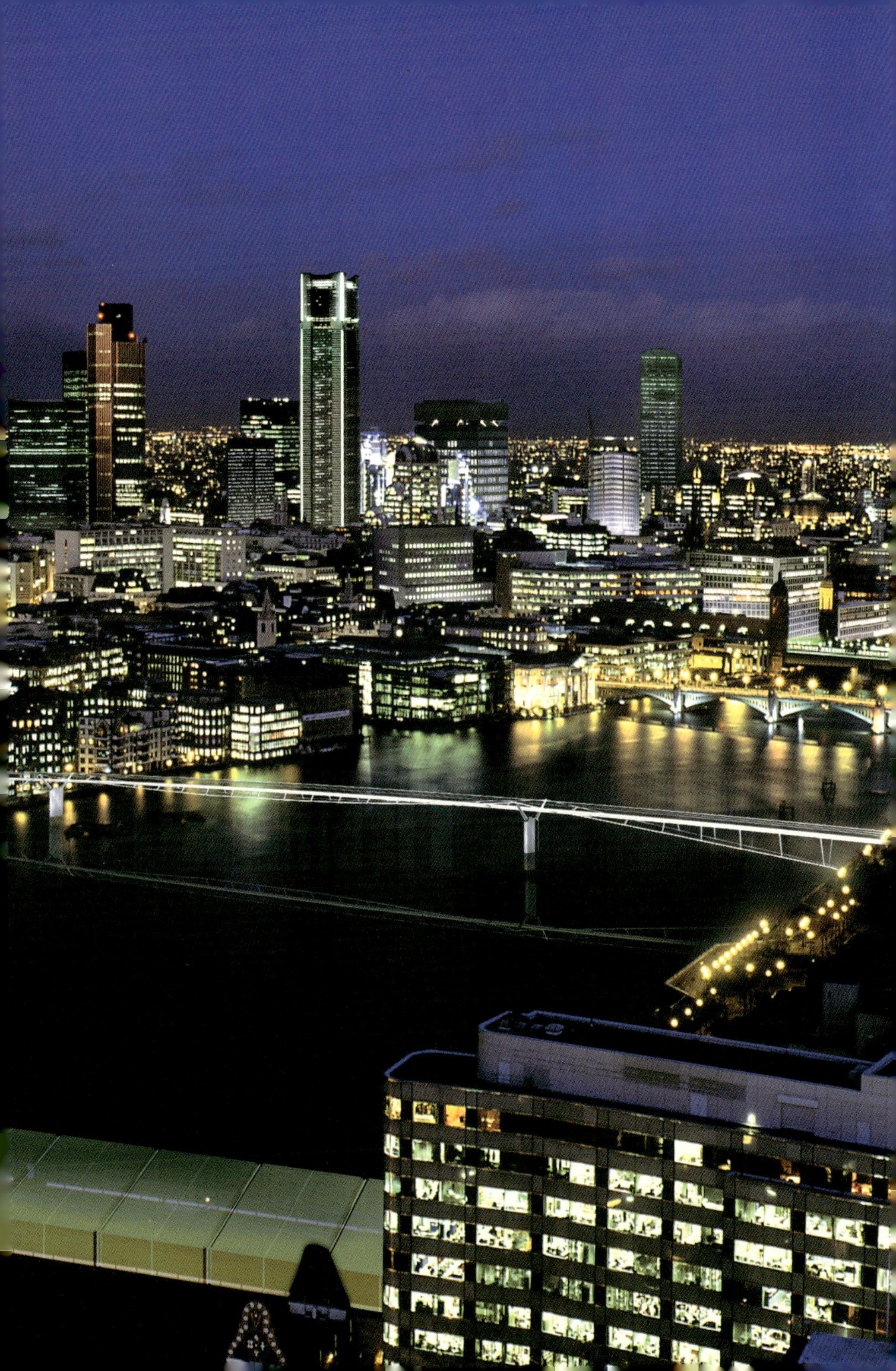

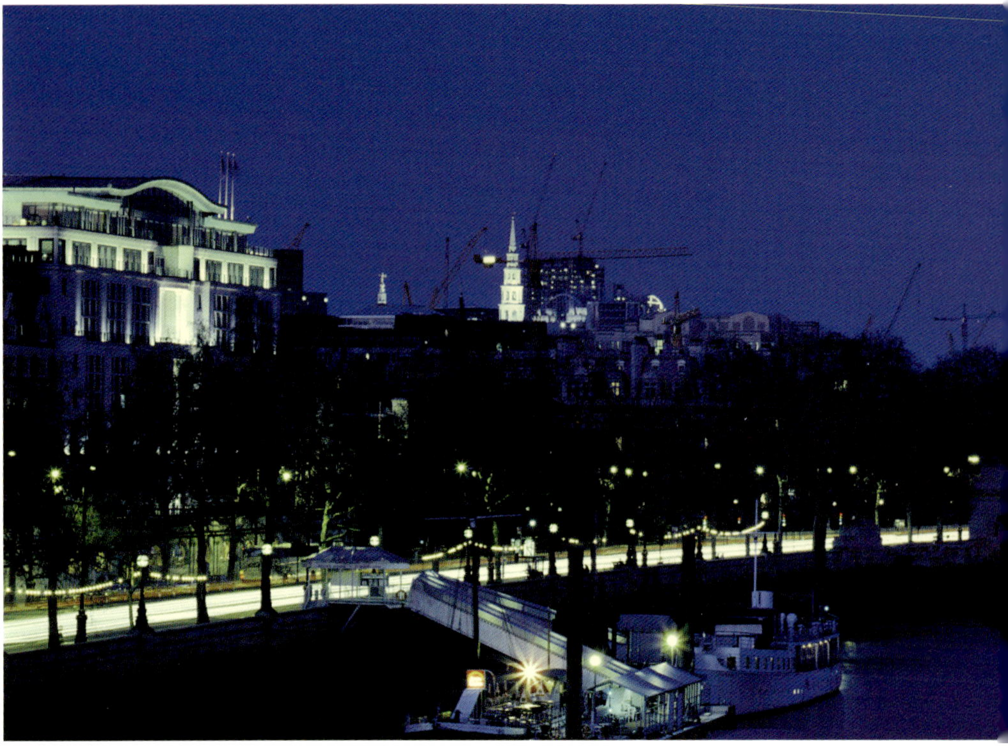

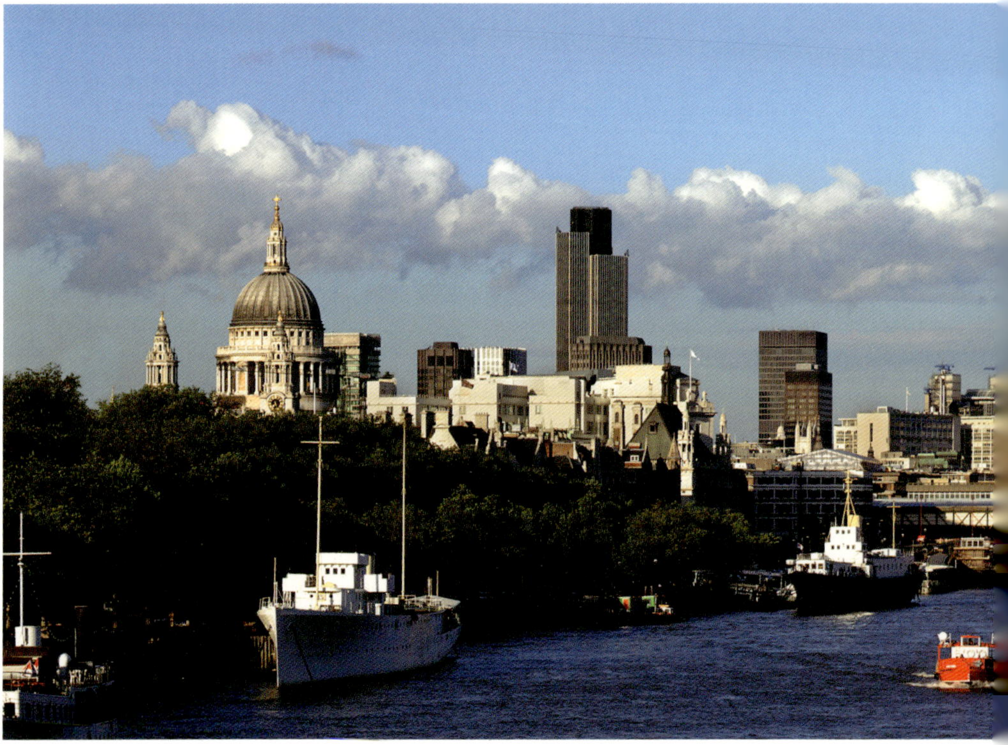

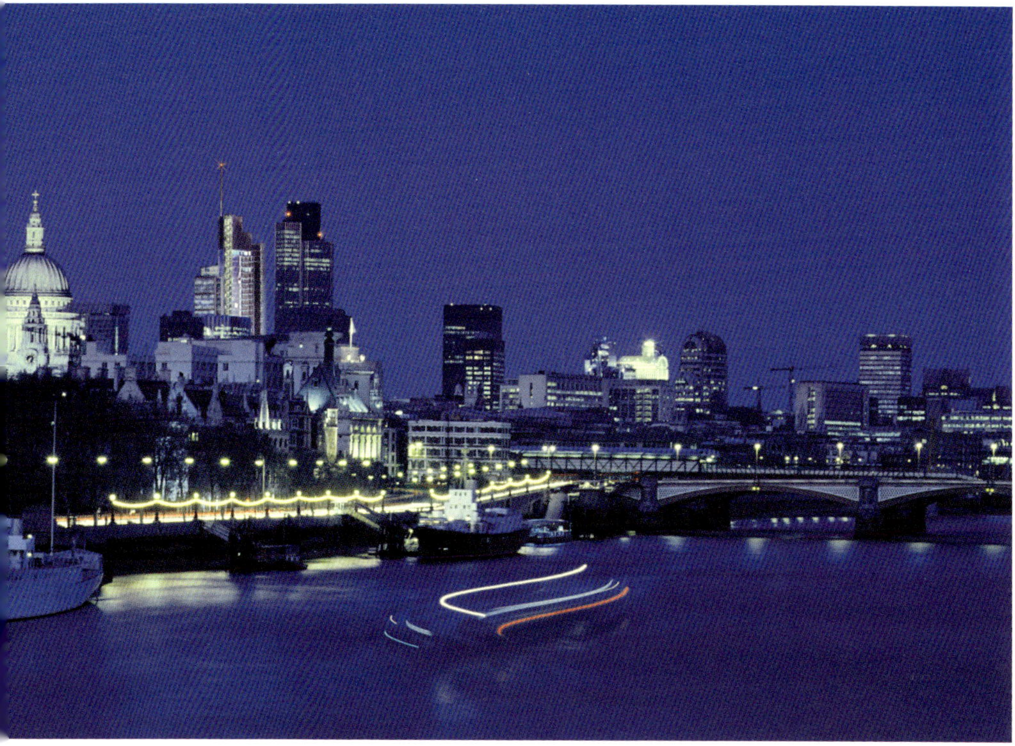

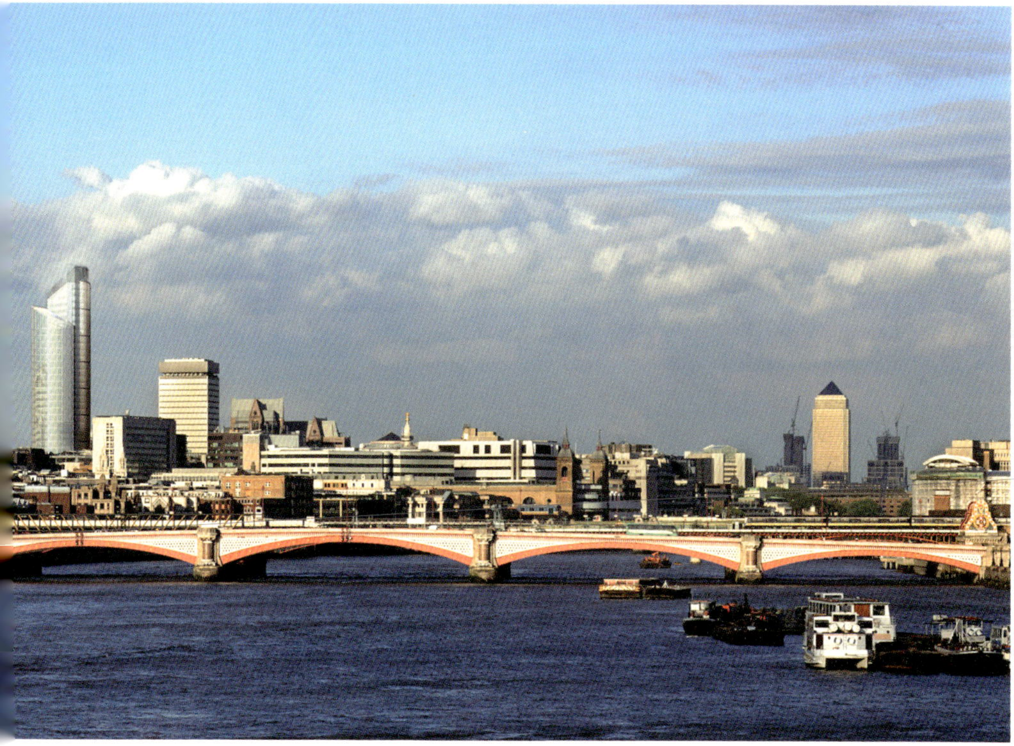

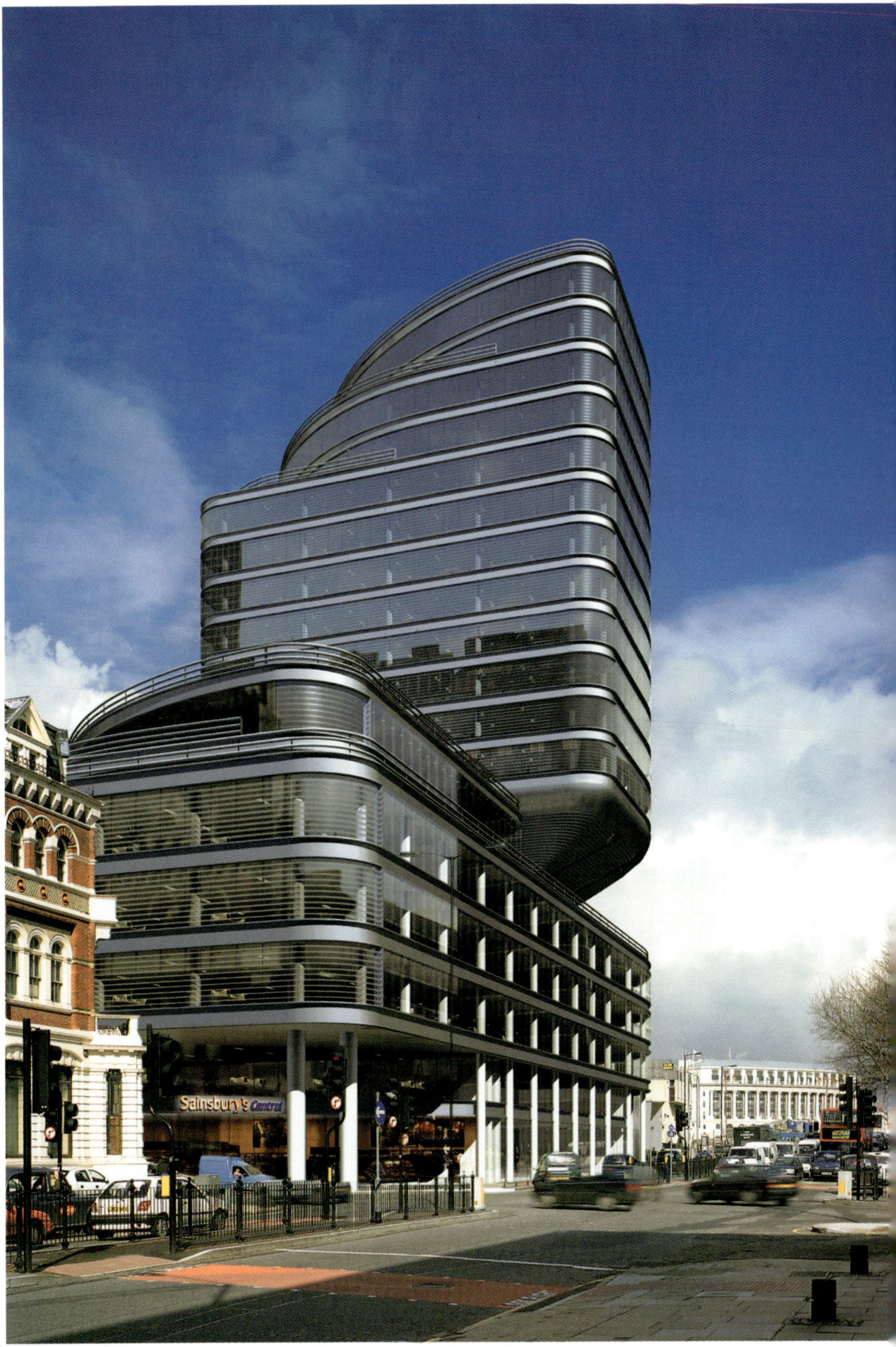
Sainsbury's Central

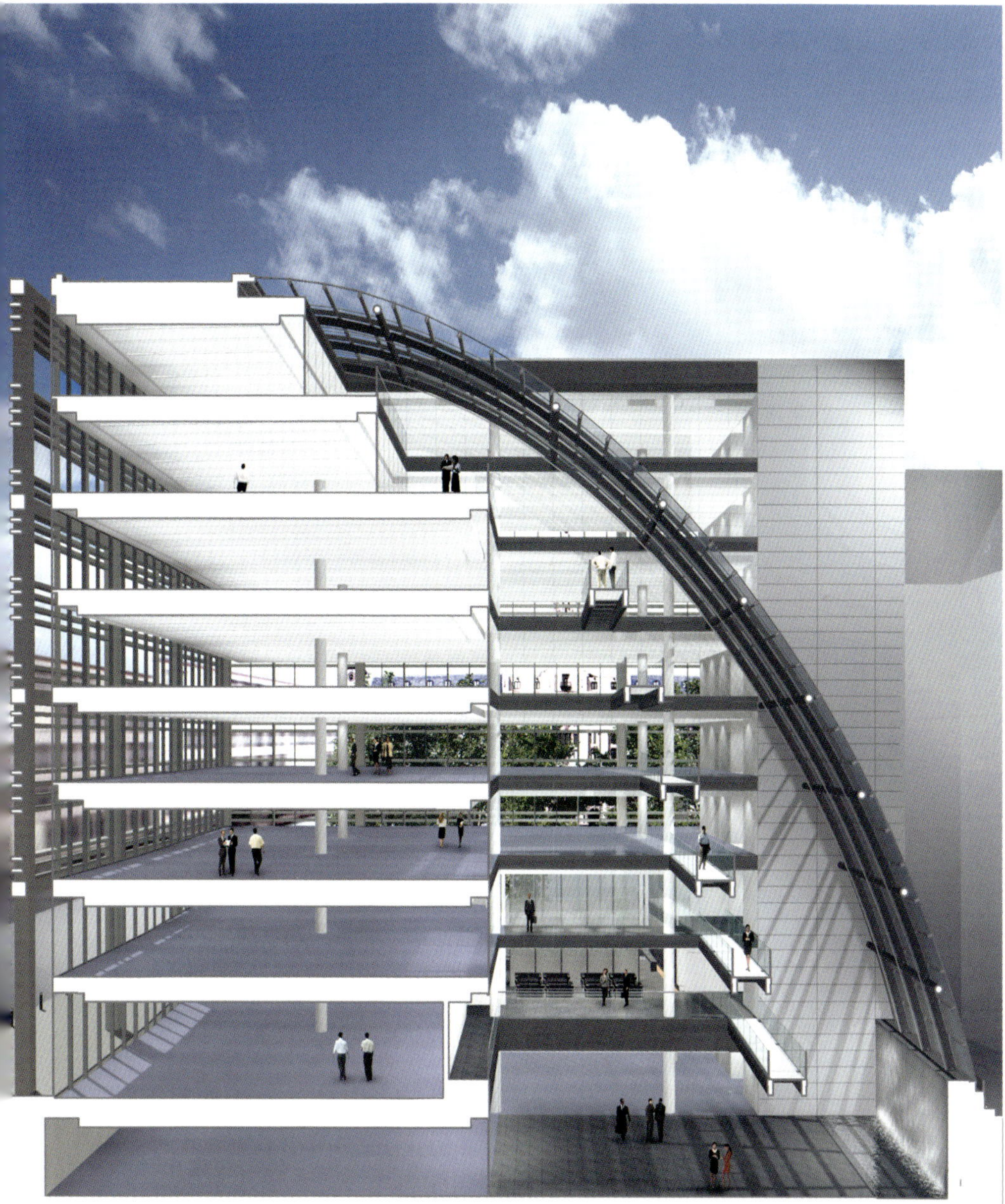

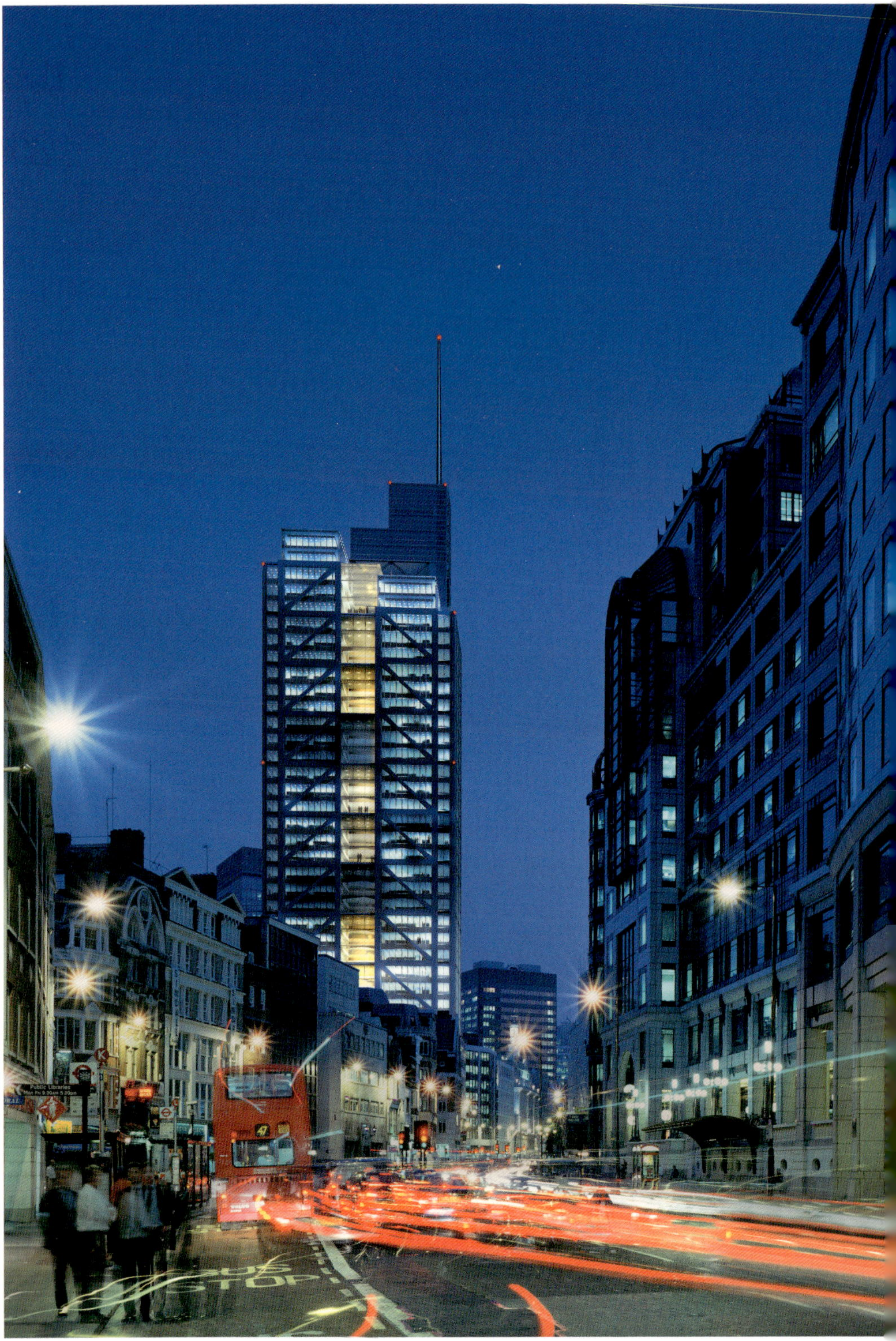
Public Libraries

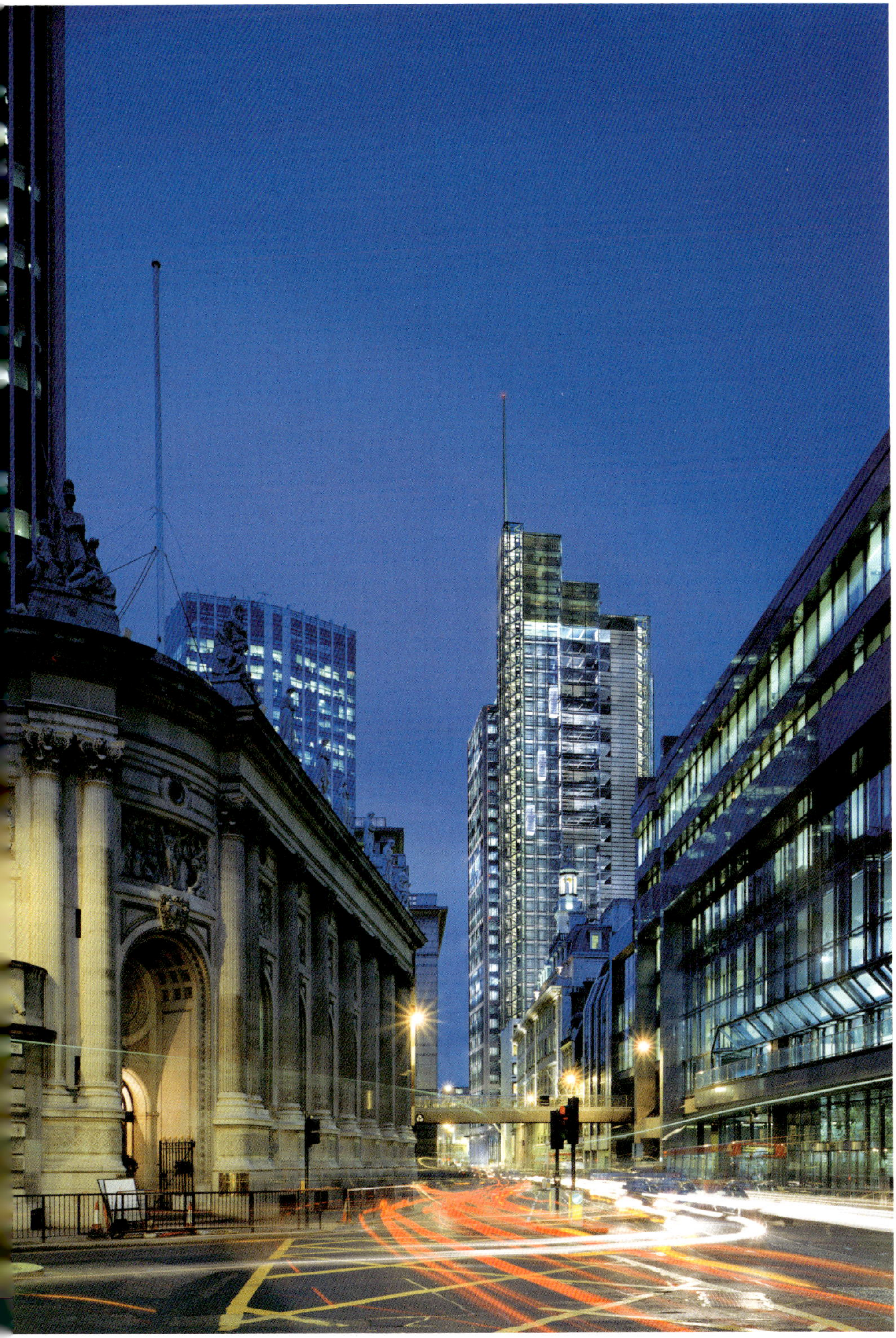

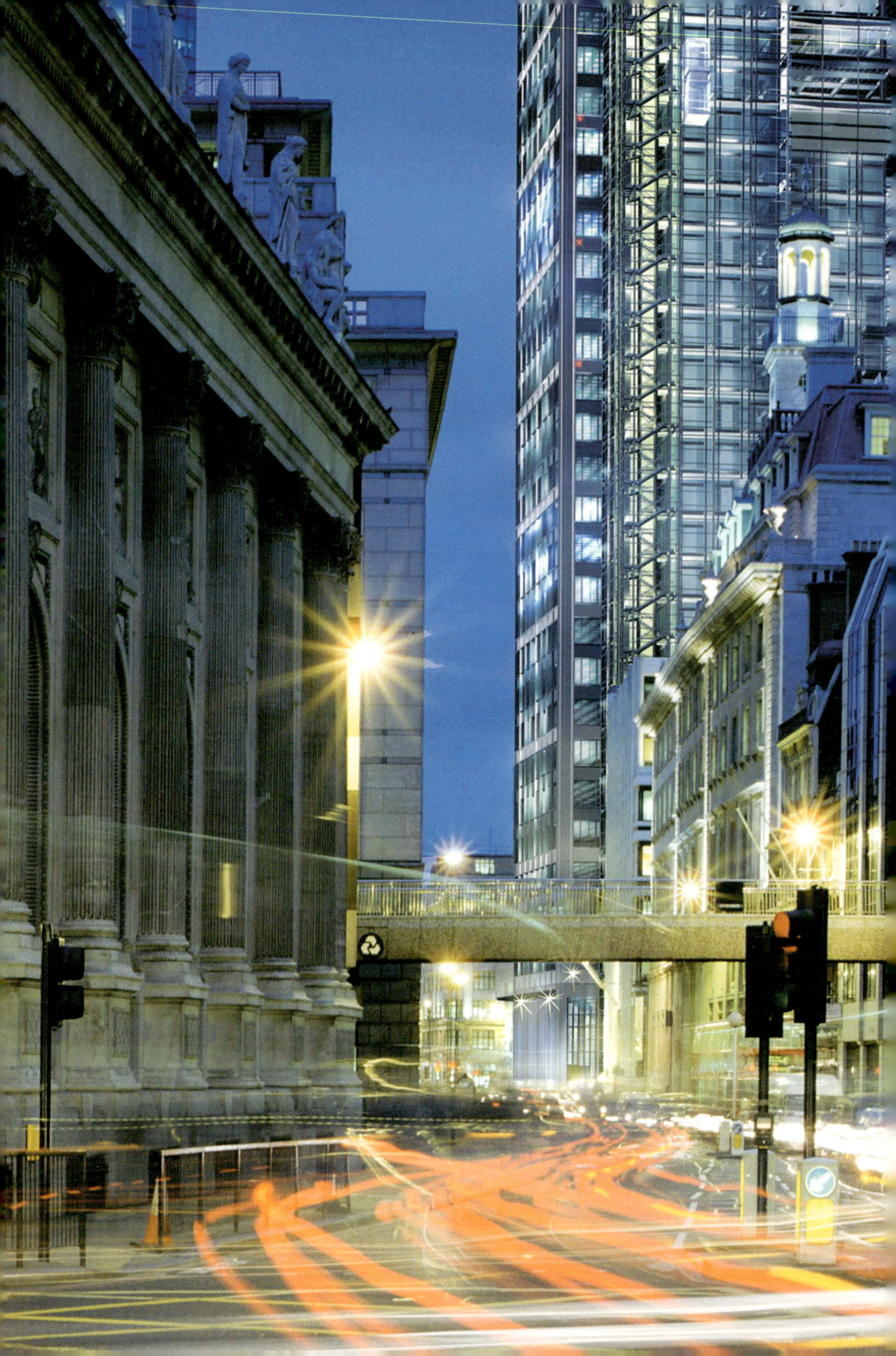

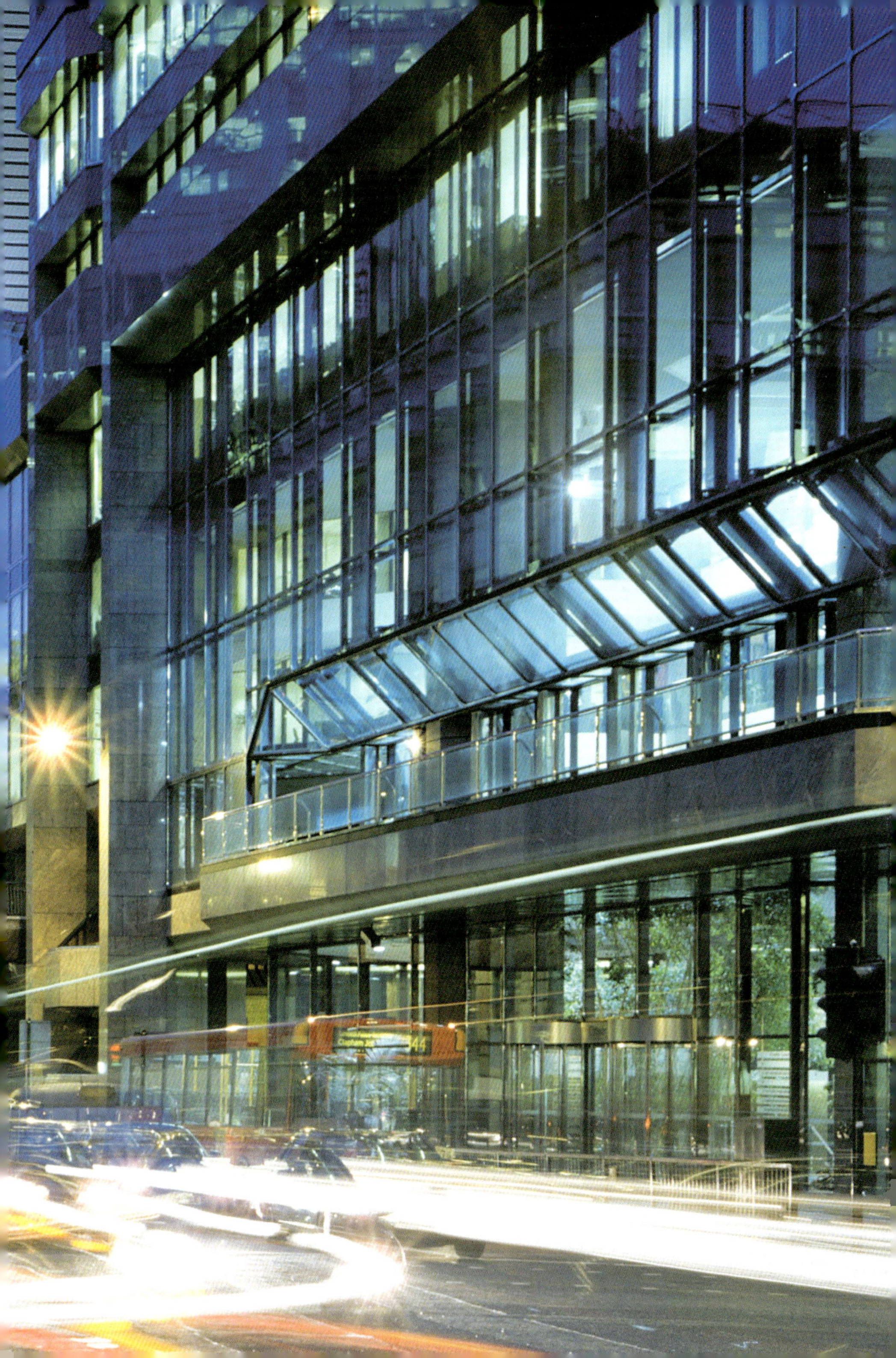

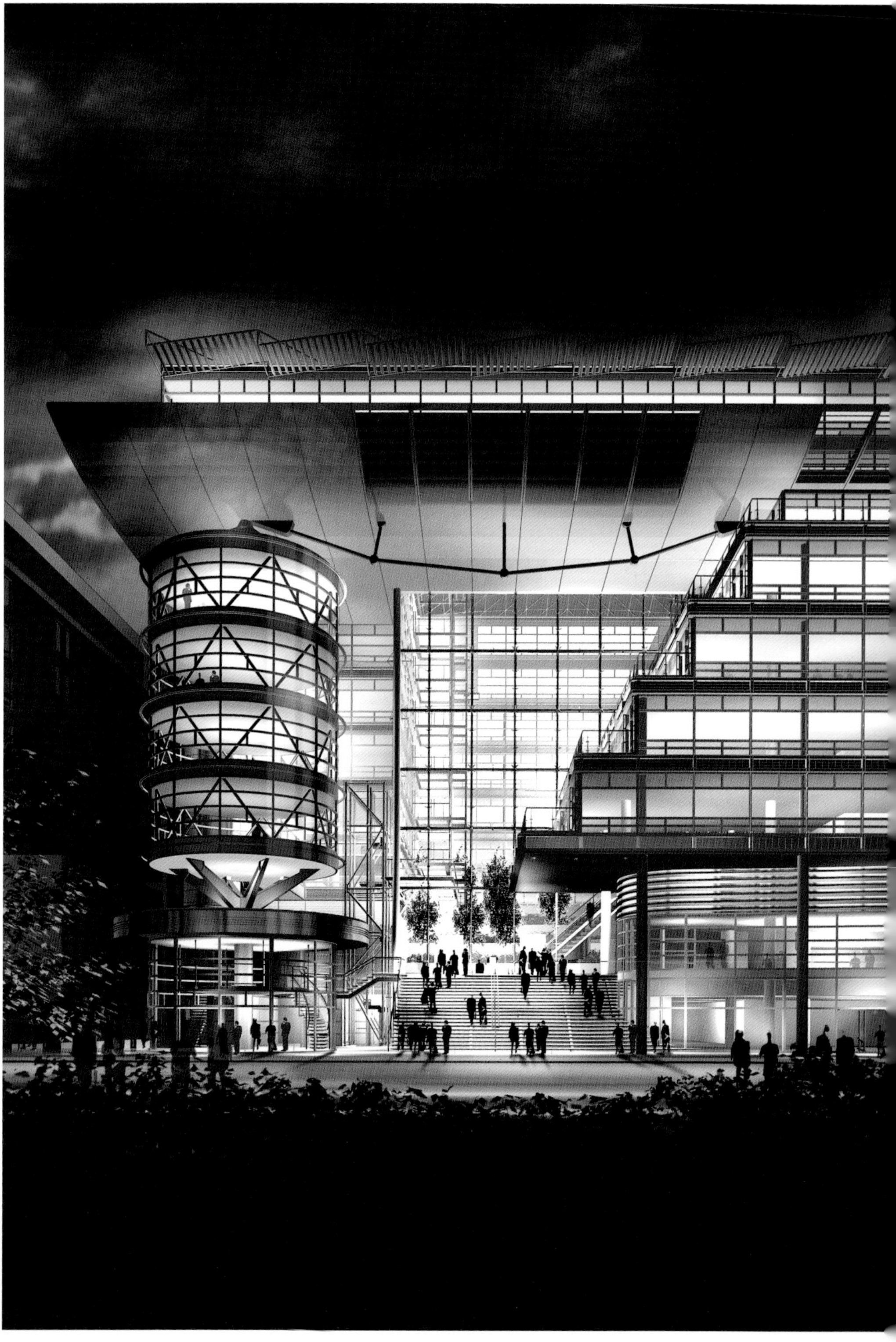

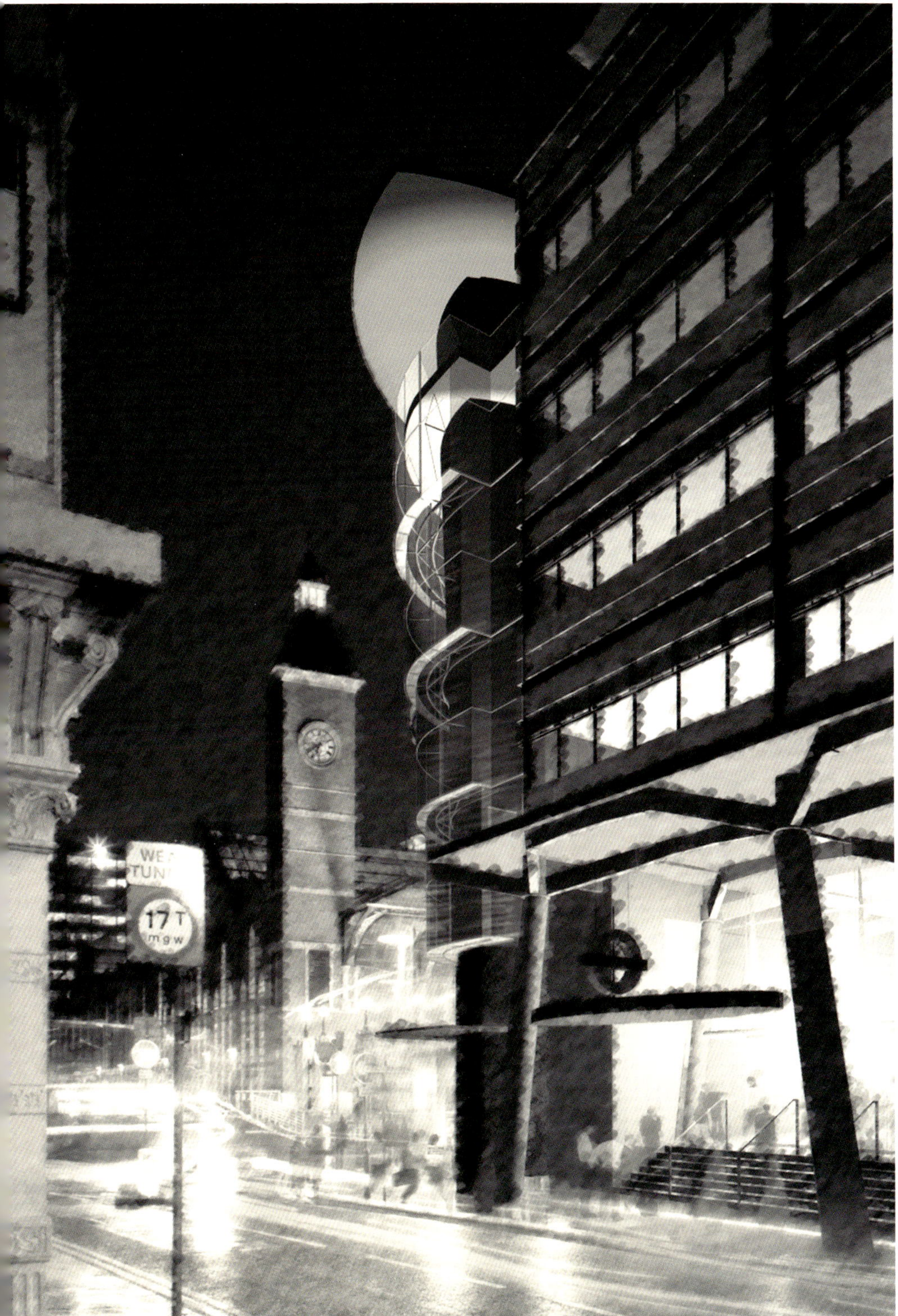
17 T
m g w

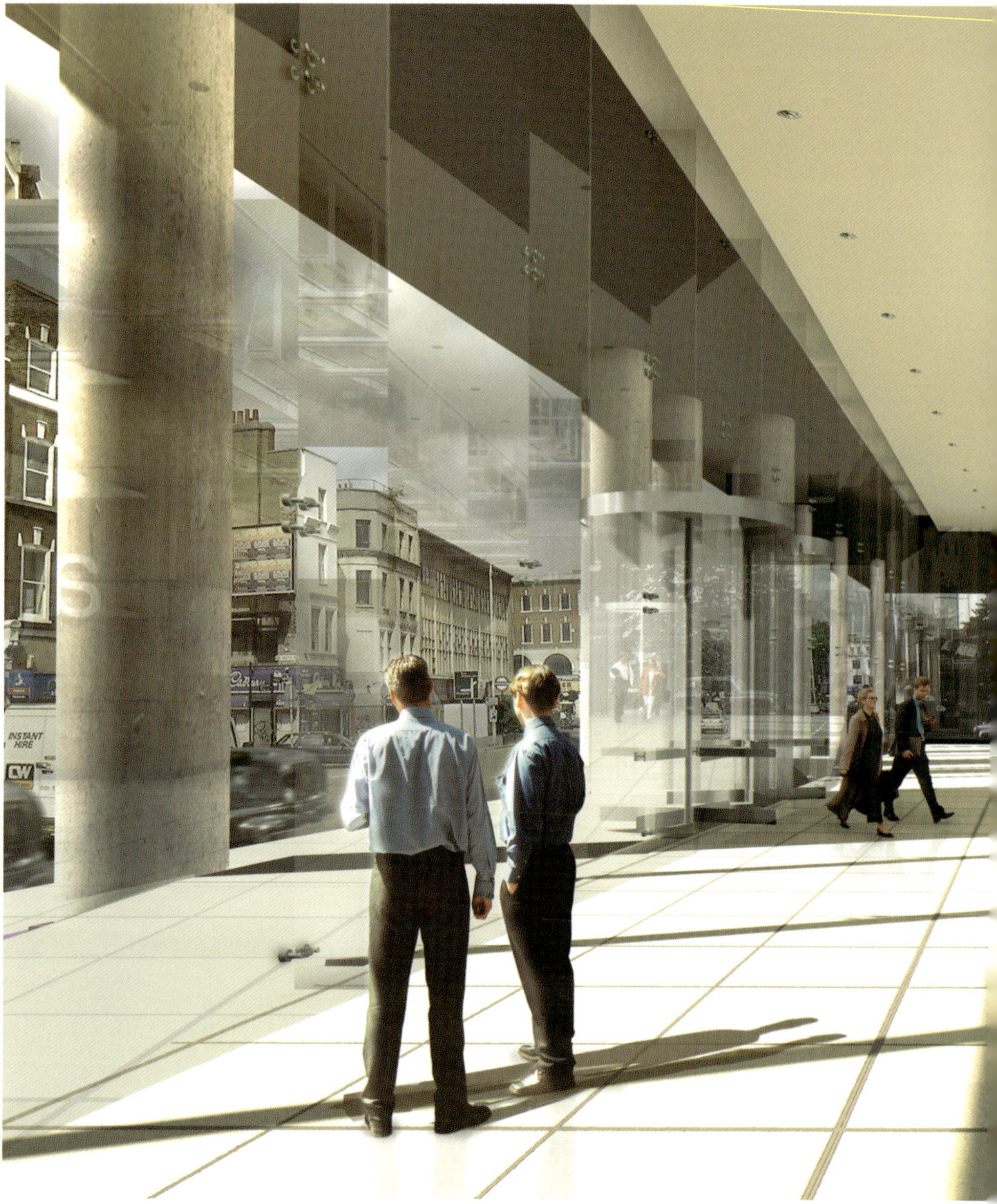
INSTANT
HIRE
CW

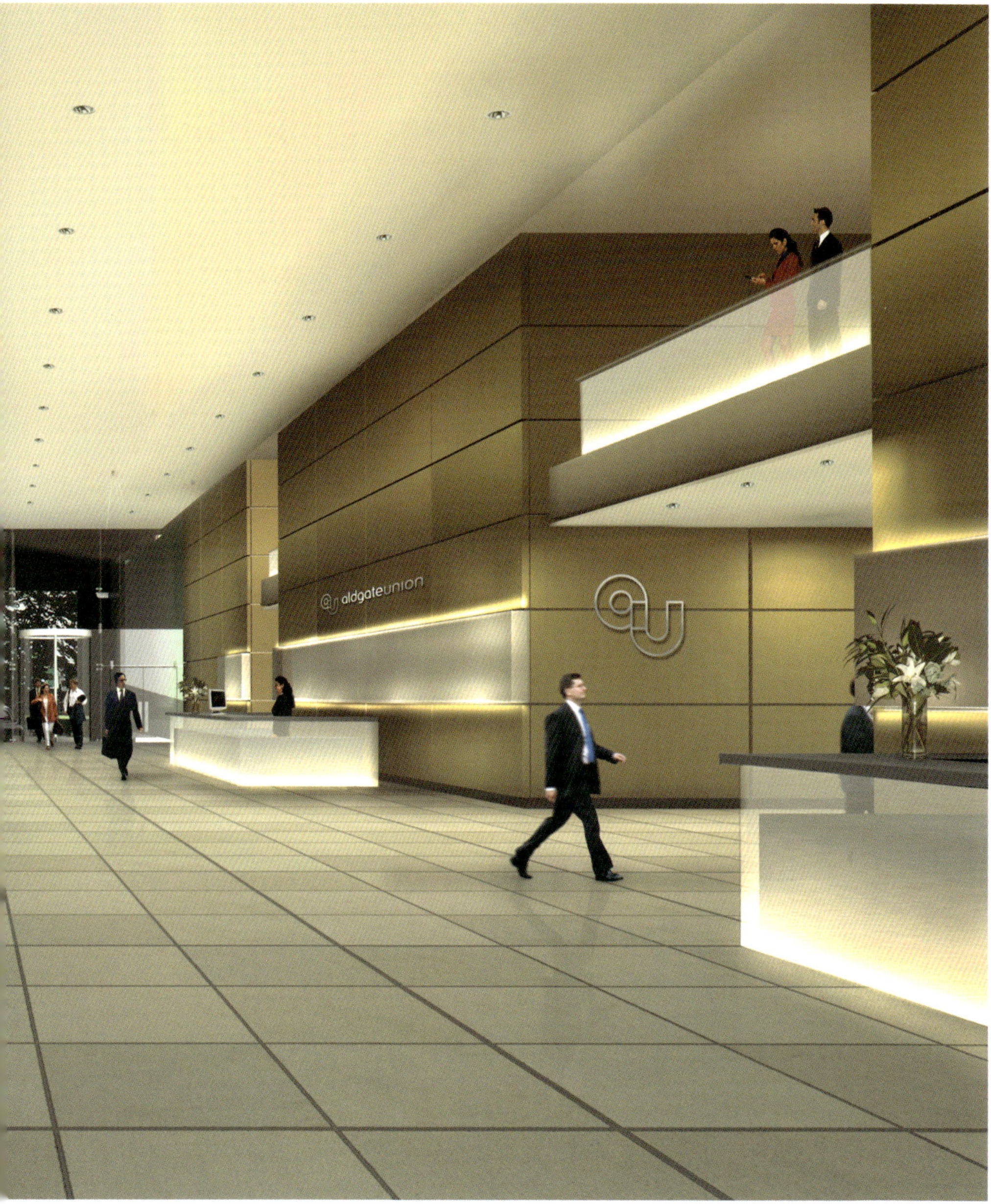
aldgateunion

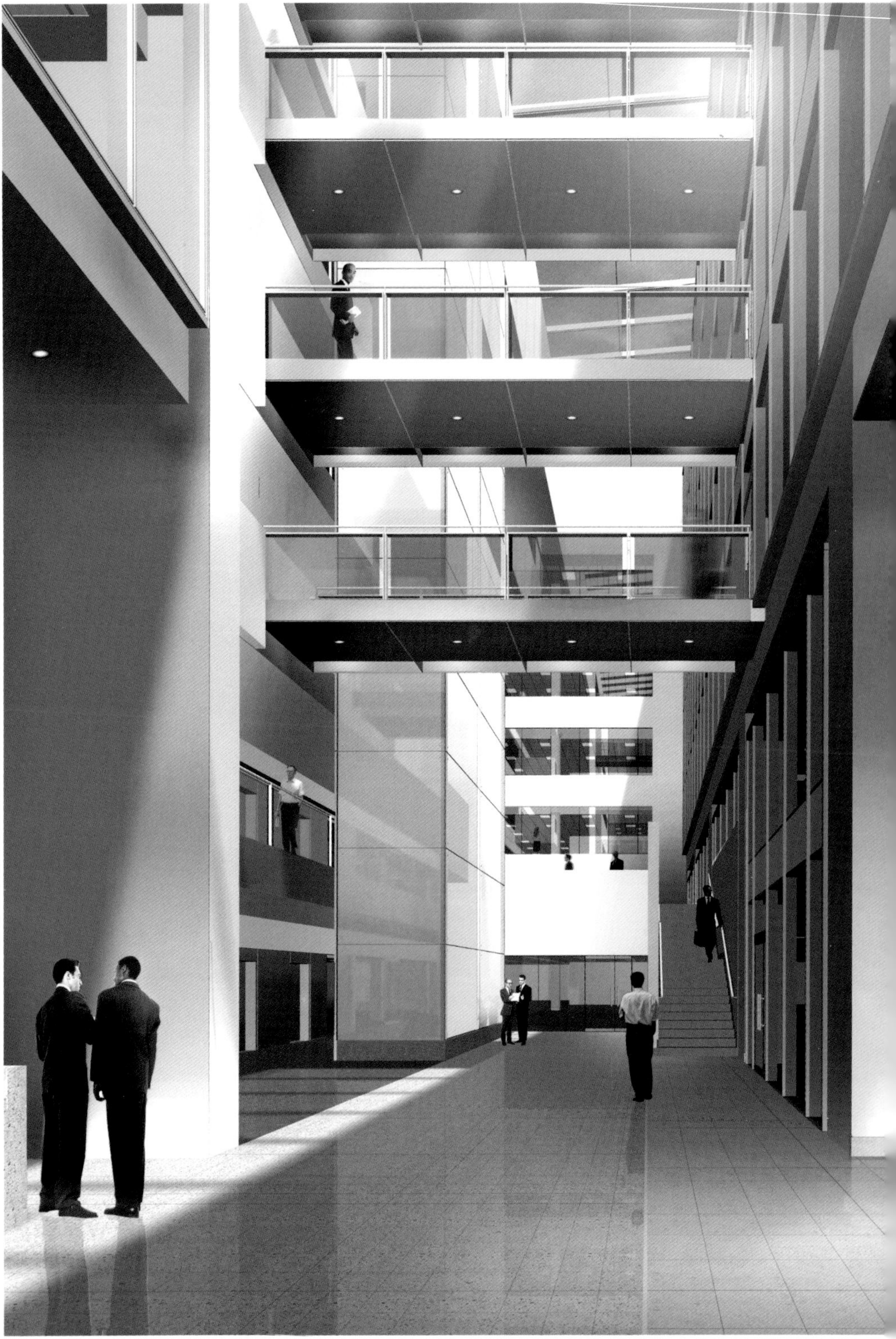

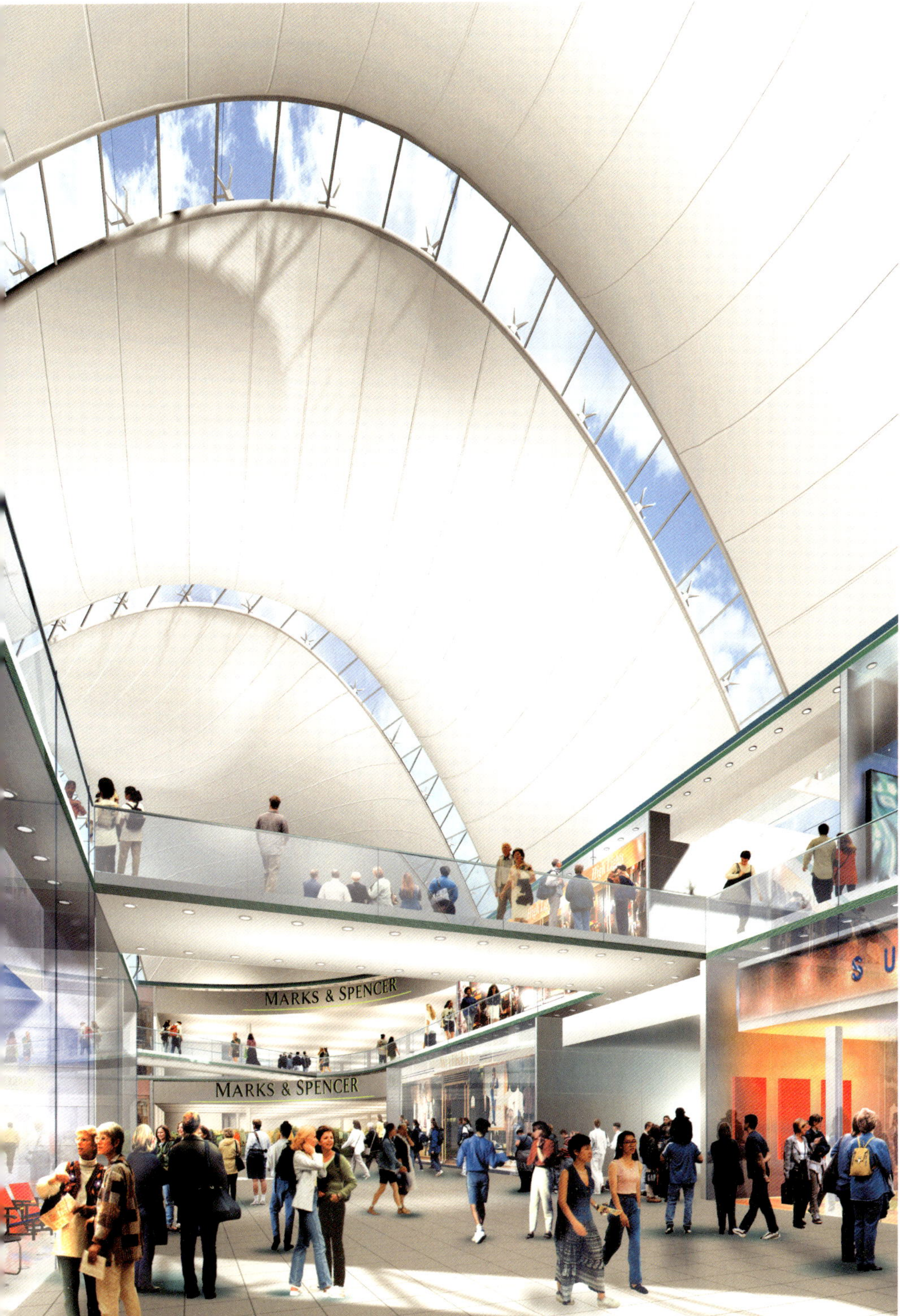
MARKS & SPENCER
MARKS & SPENCER

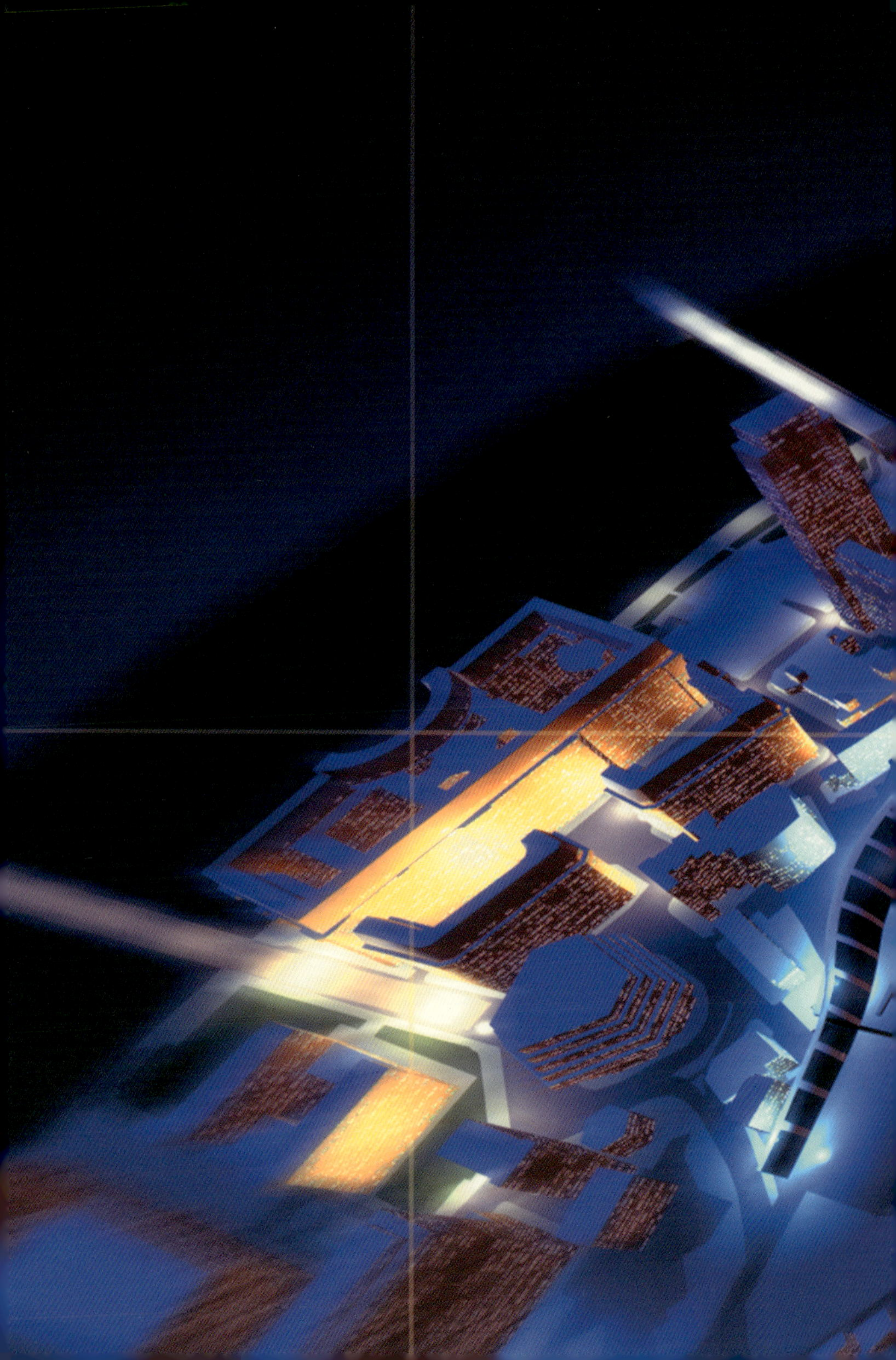

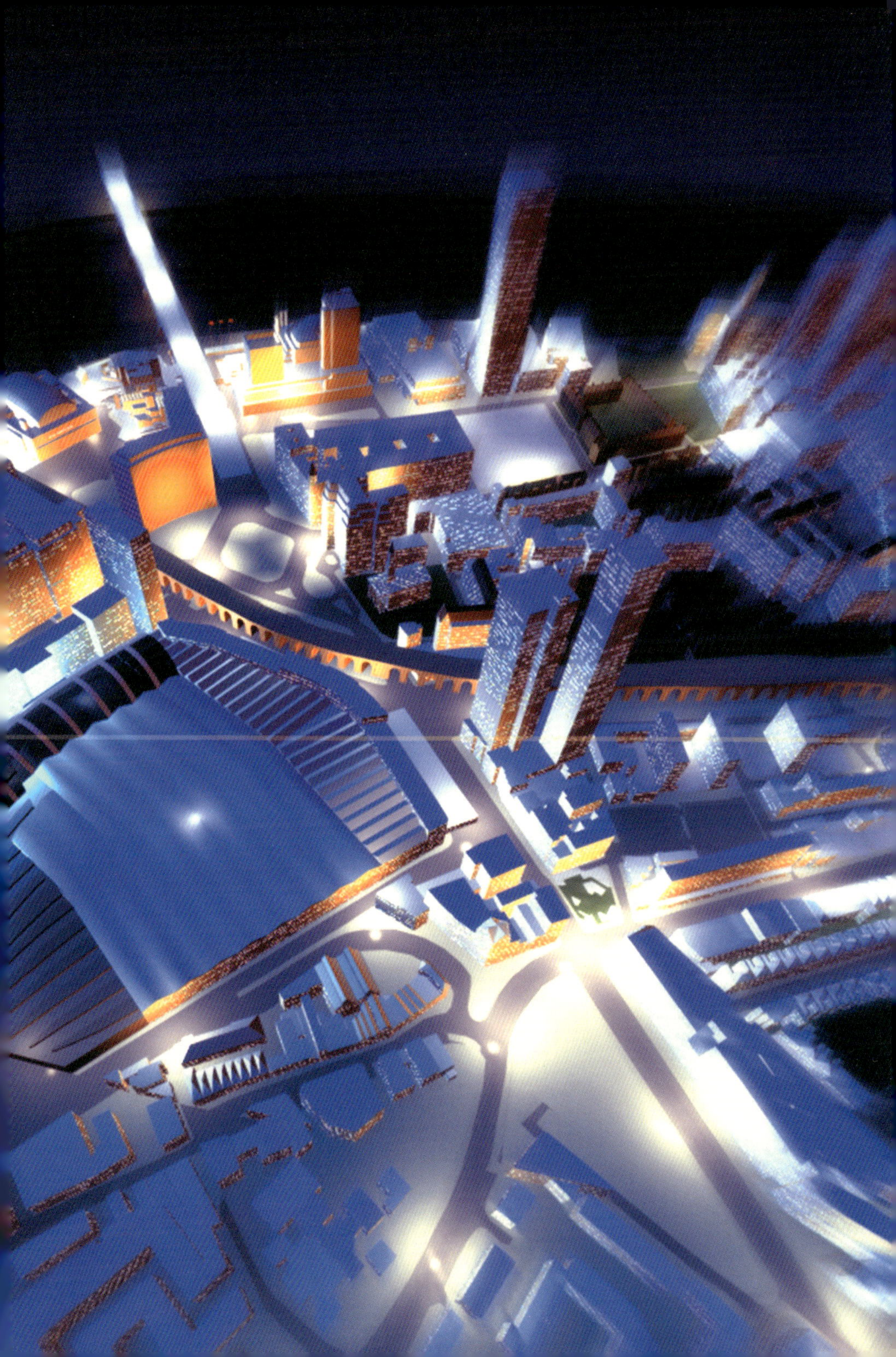

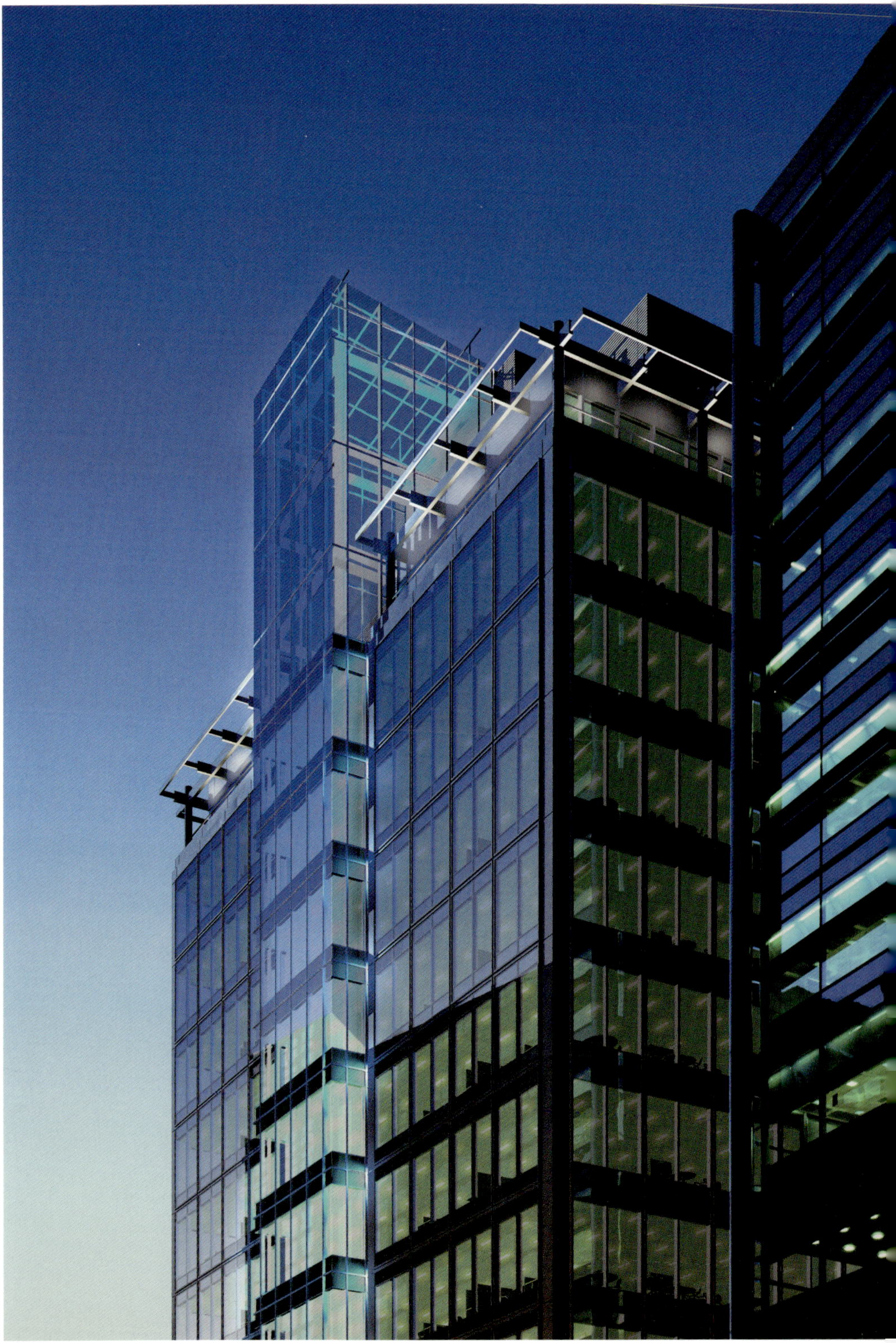

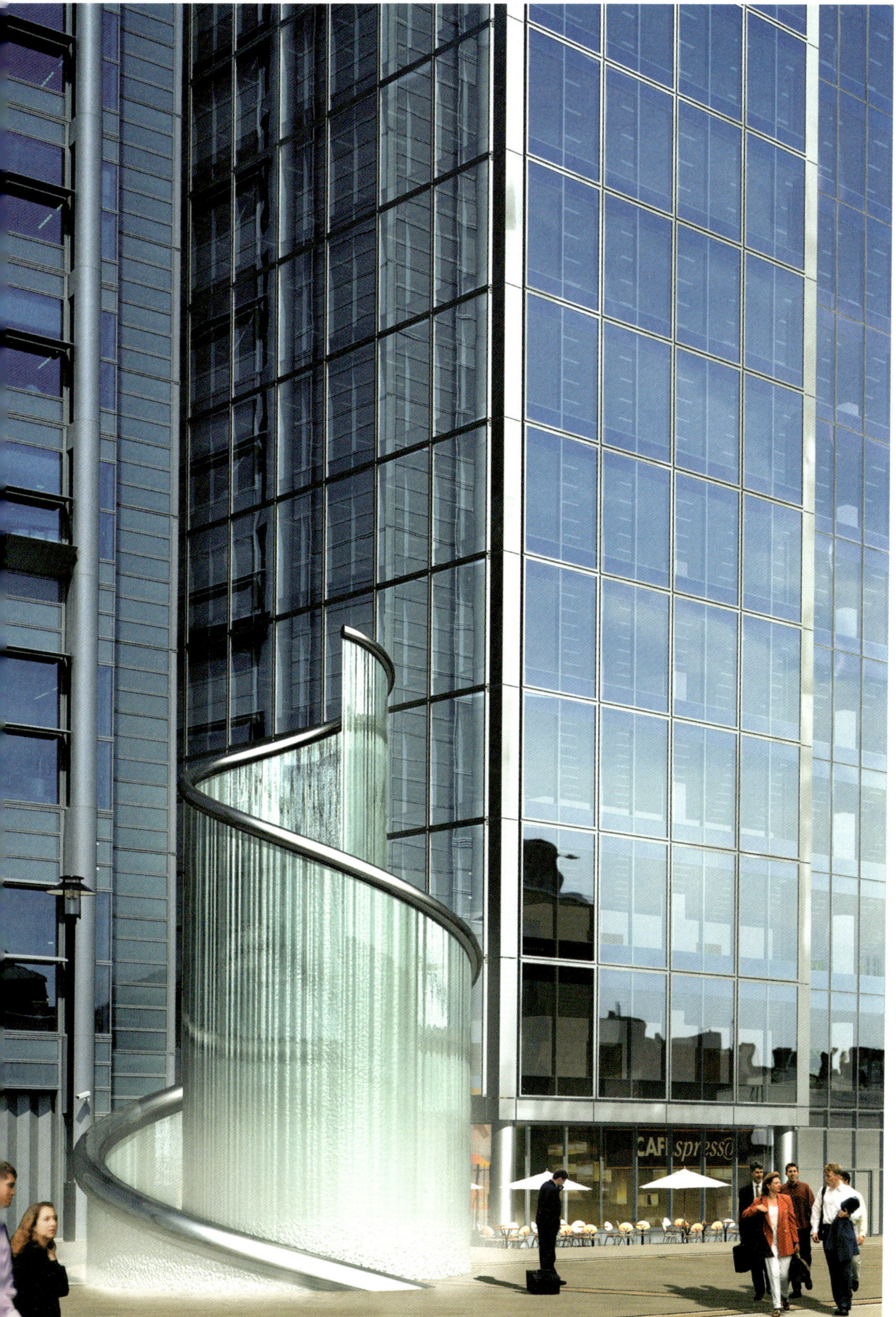
CAFE spresso

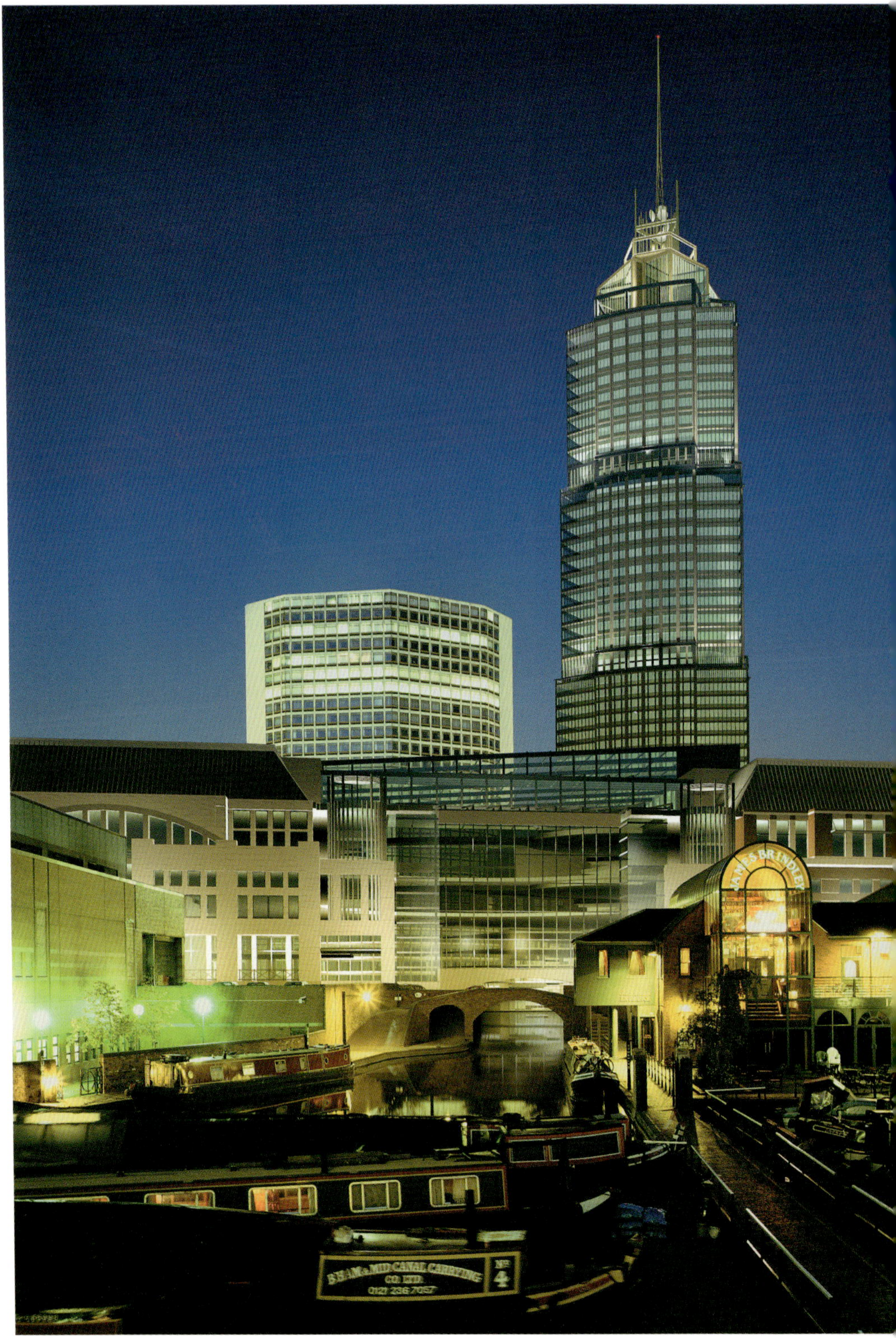
JAMES BRINDLEY

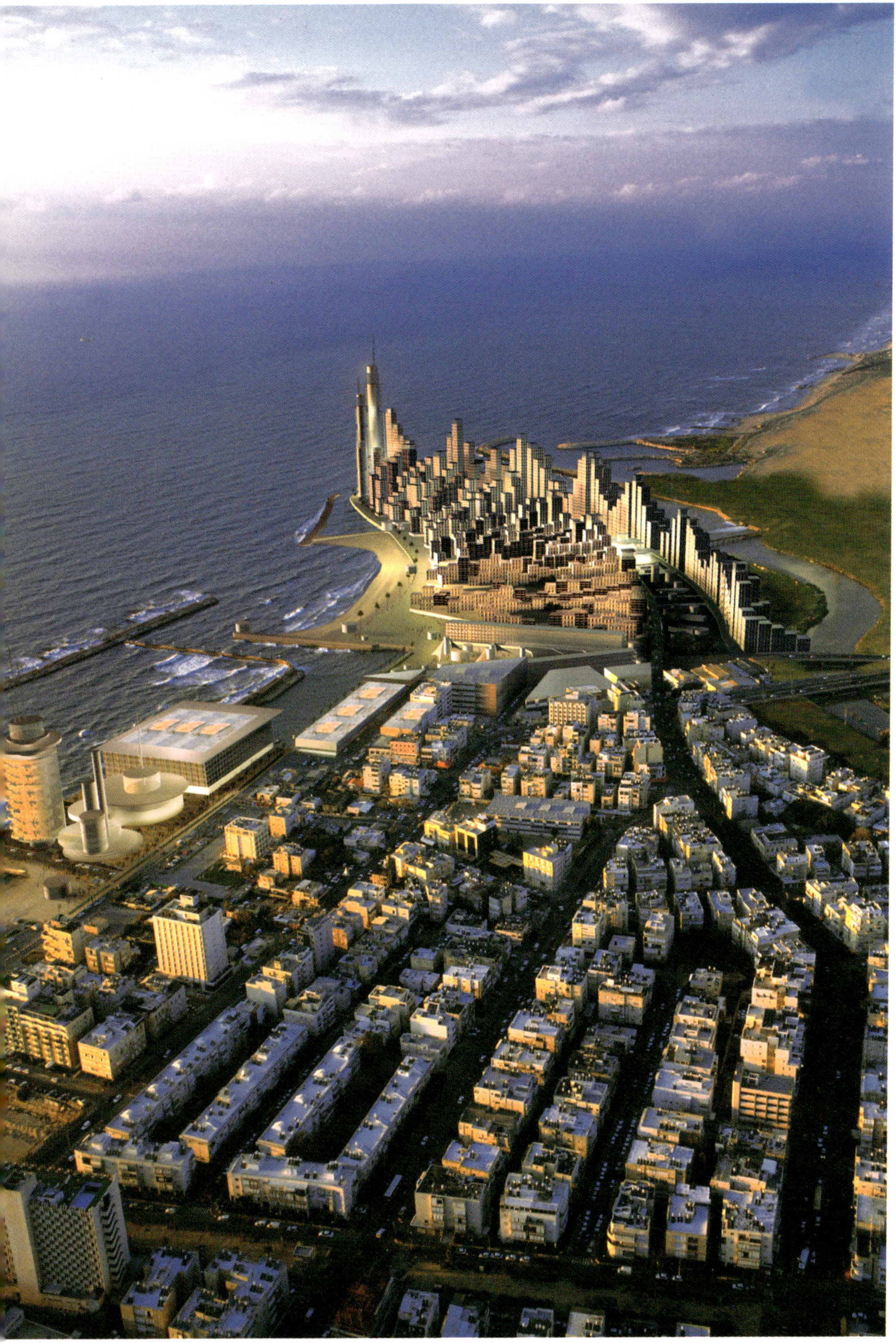

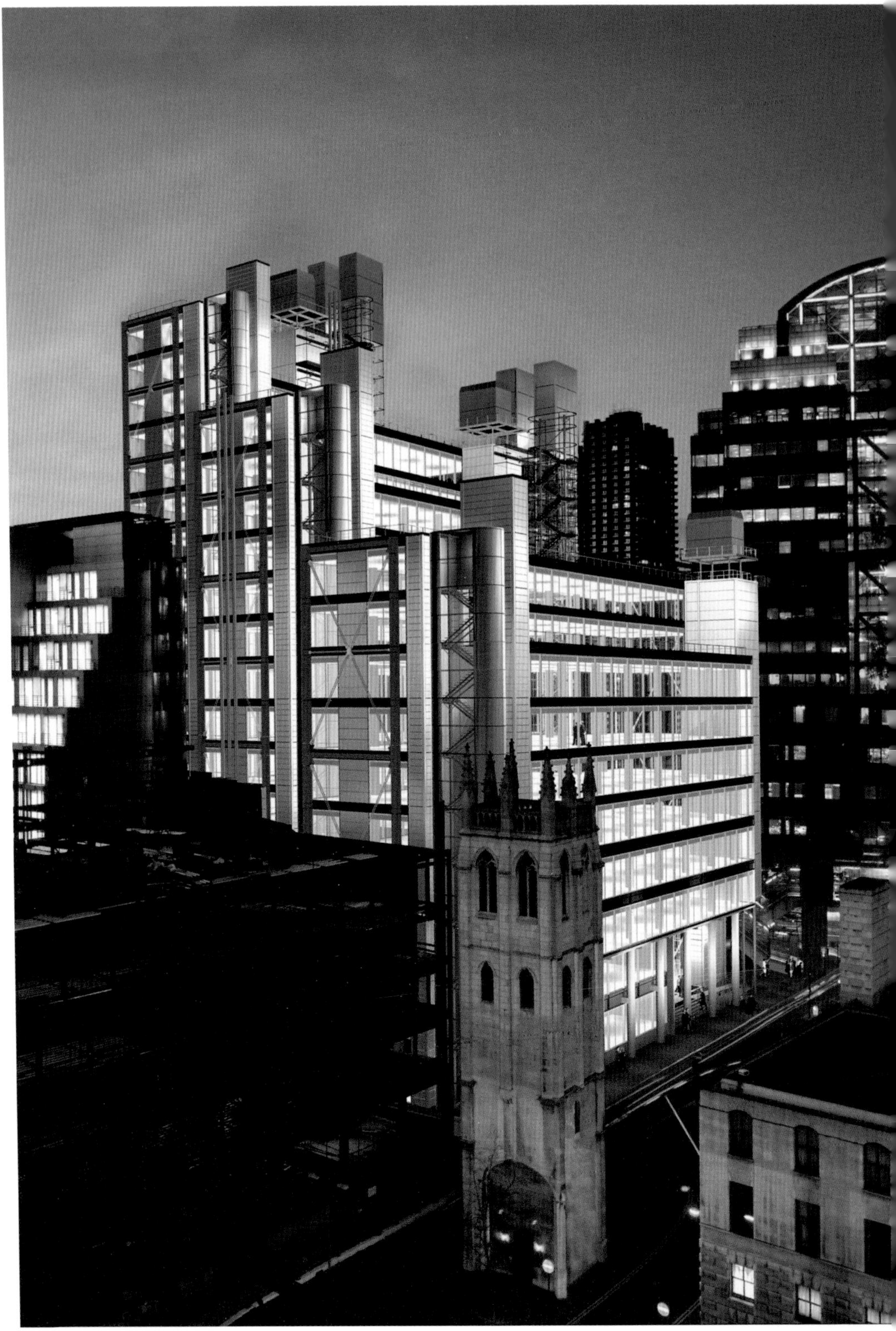

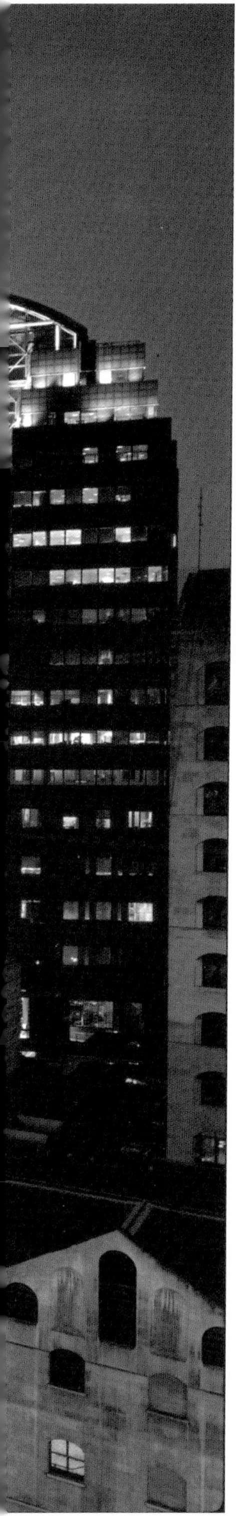

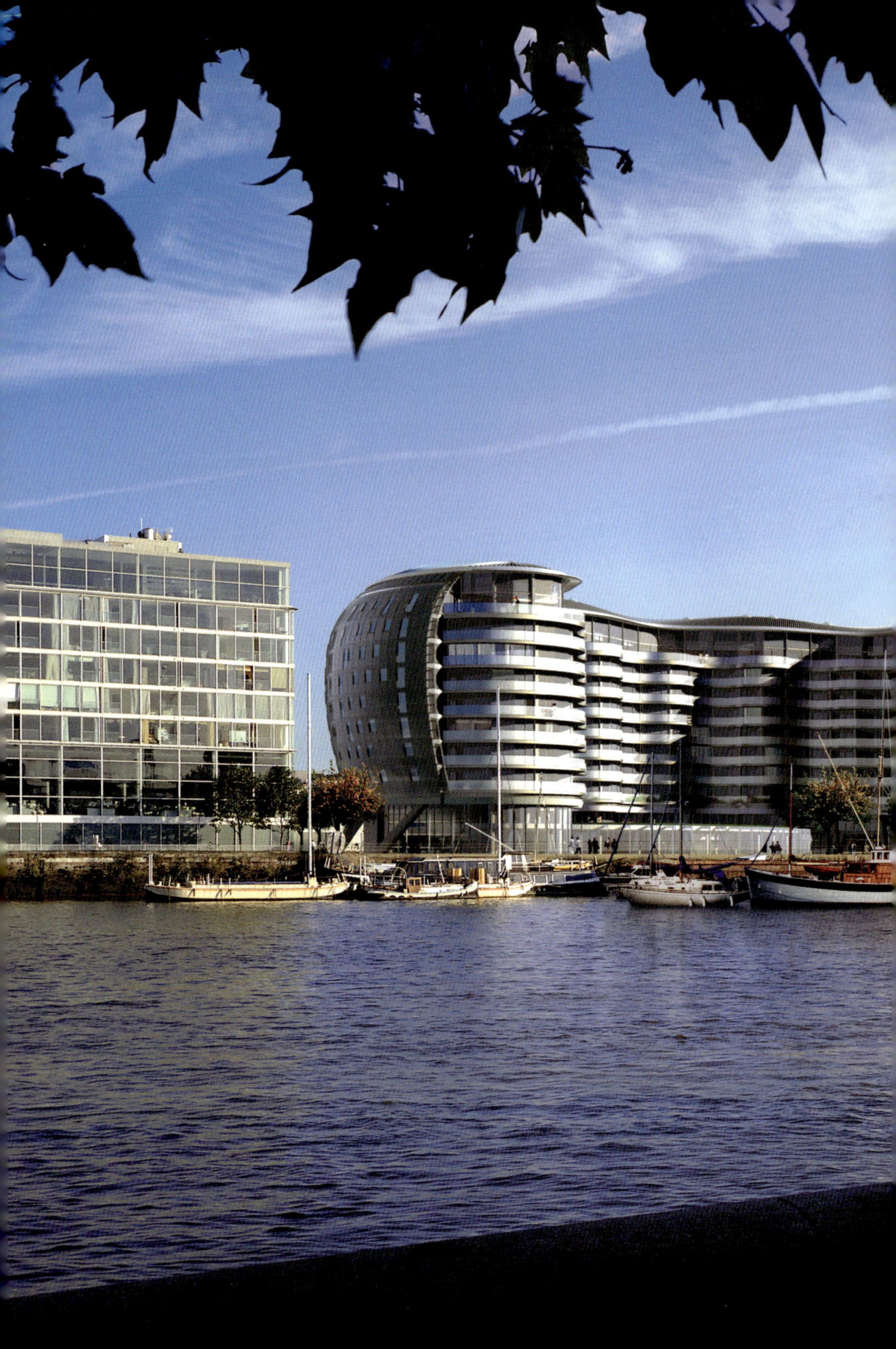

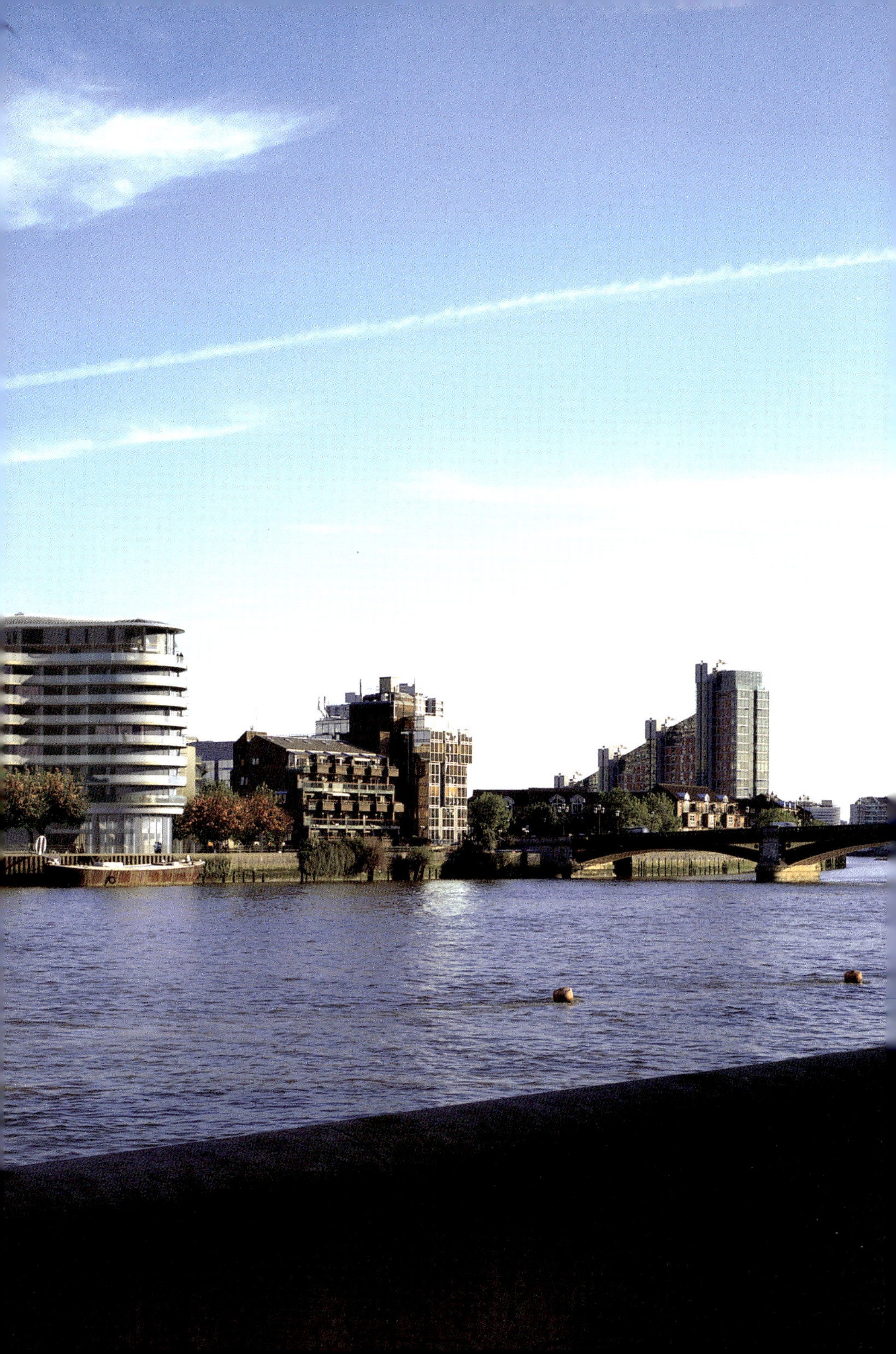

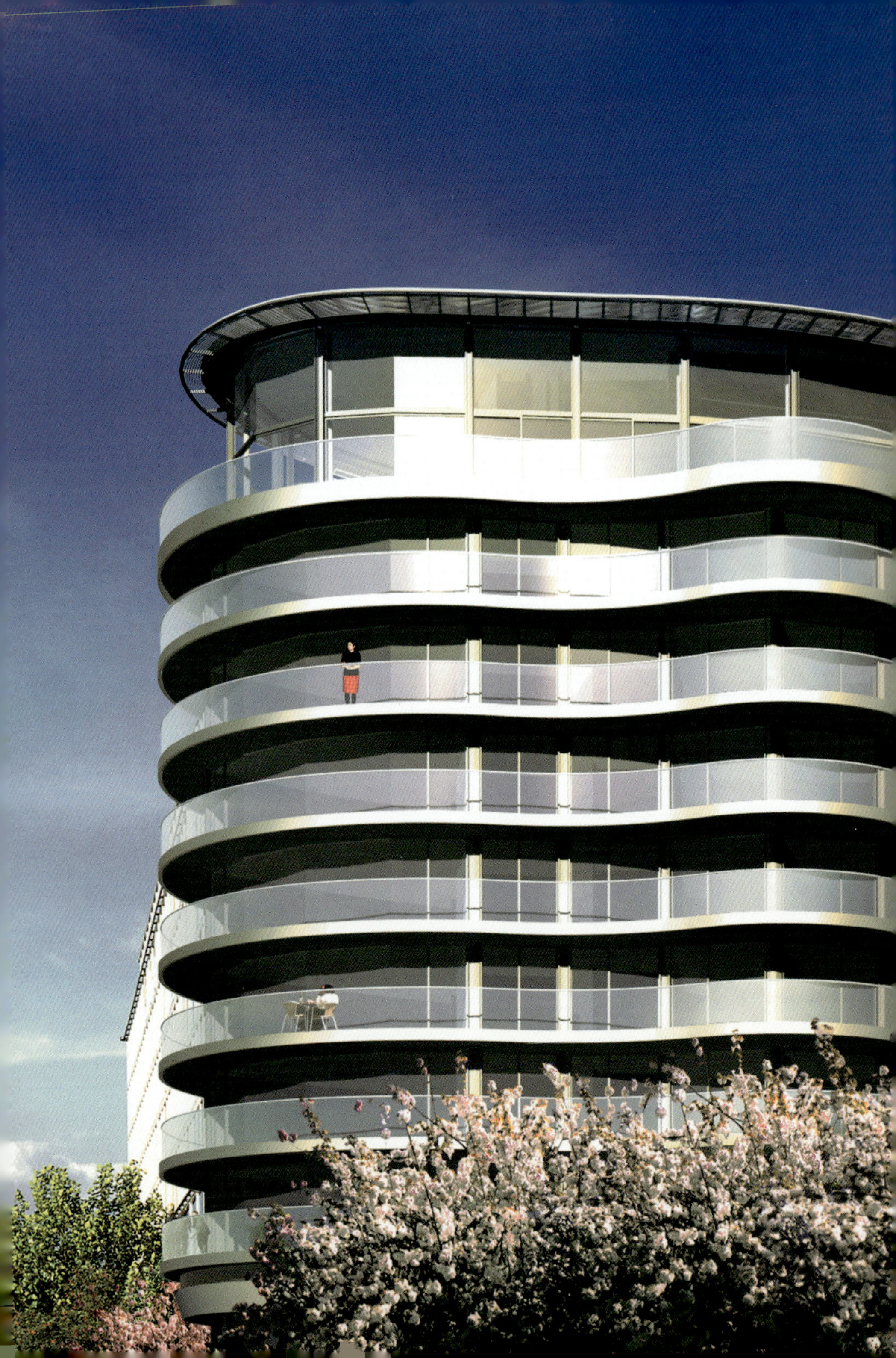

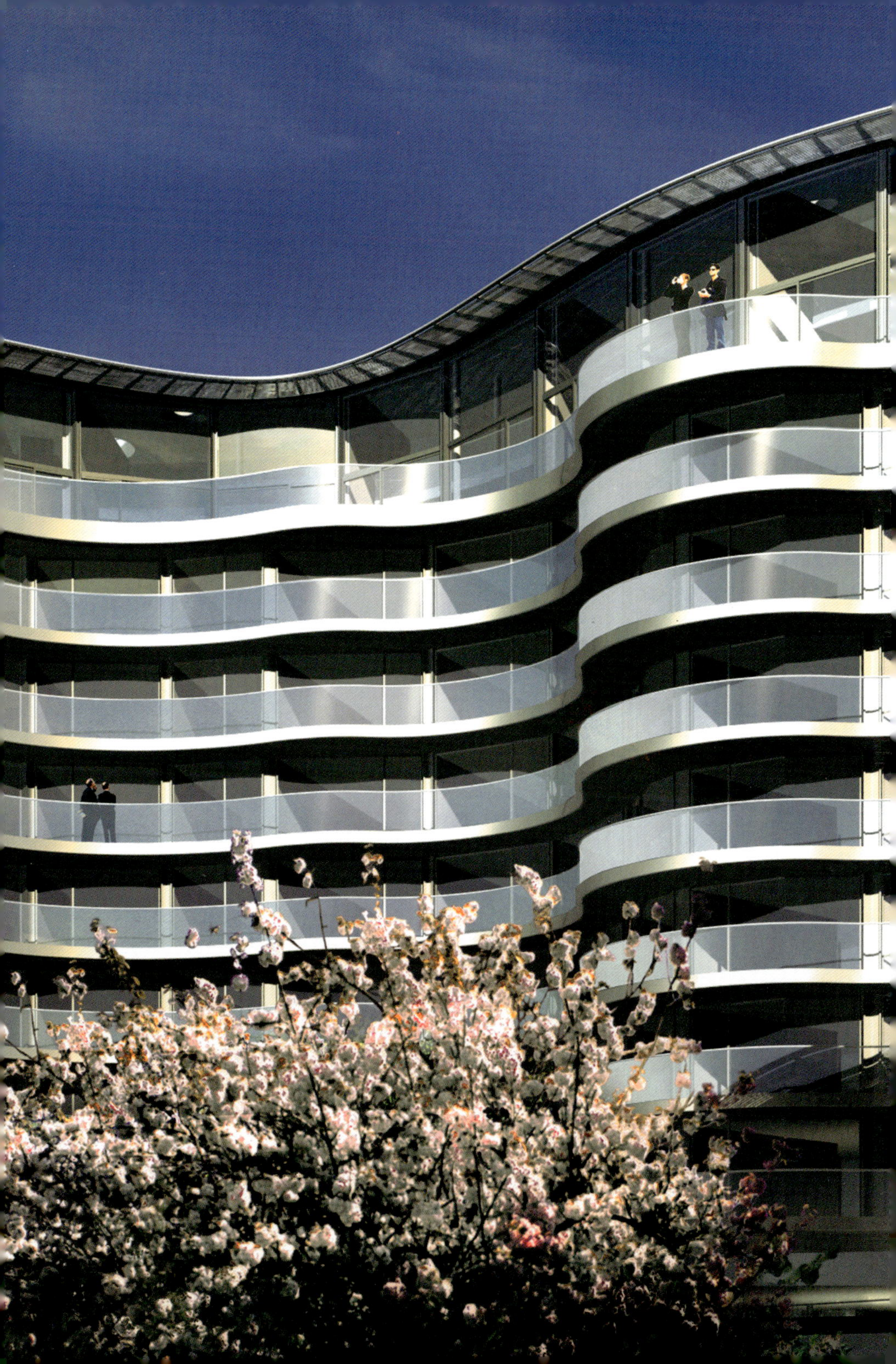

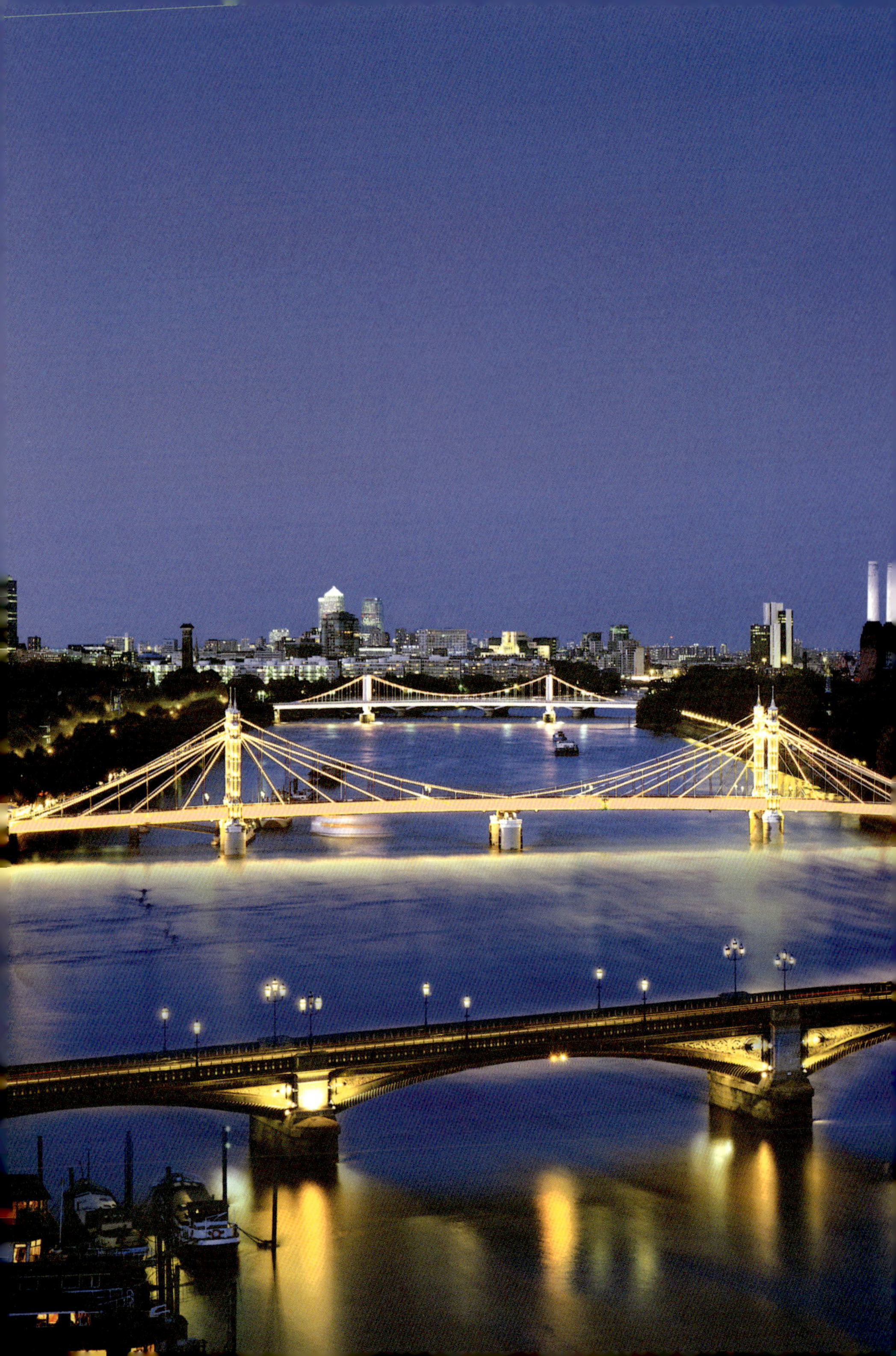

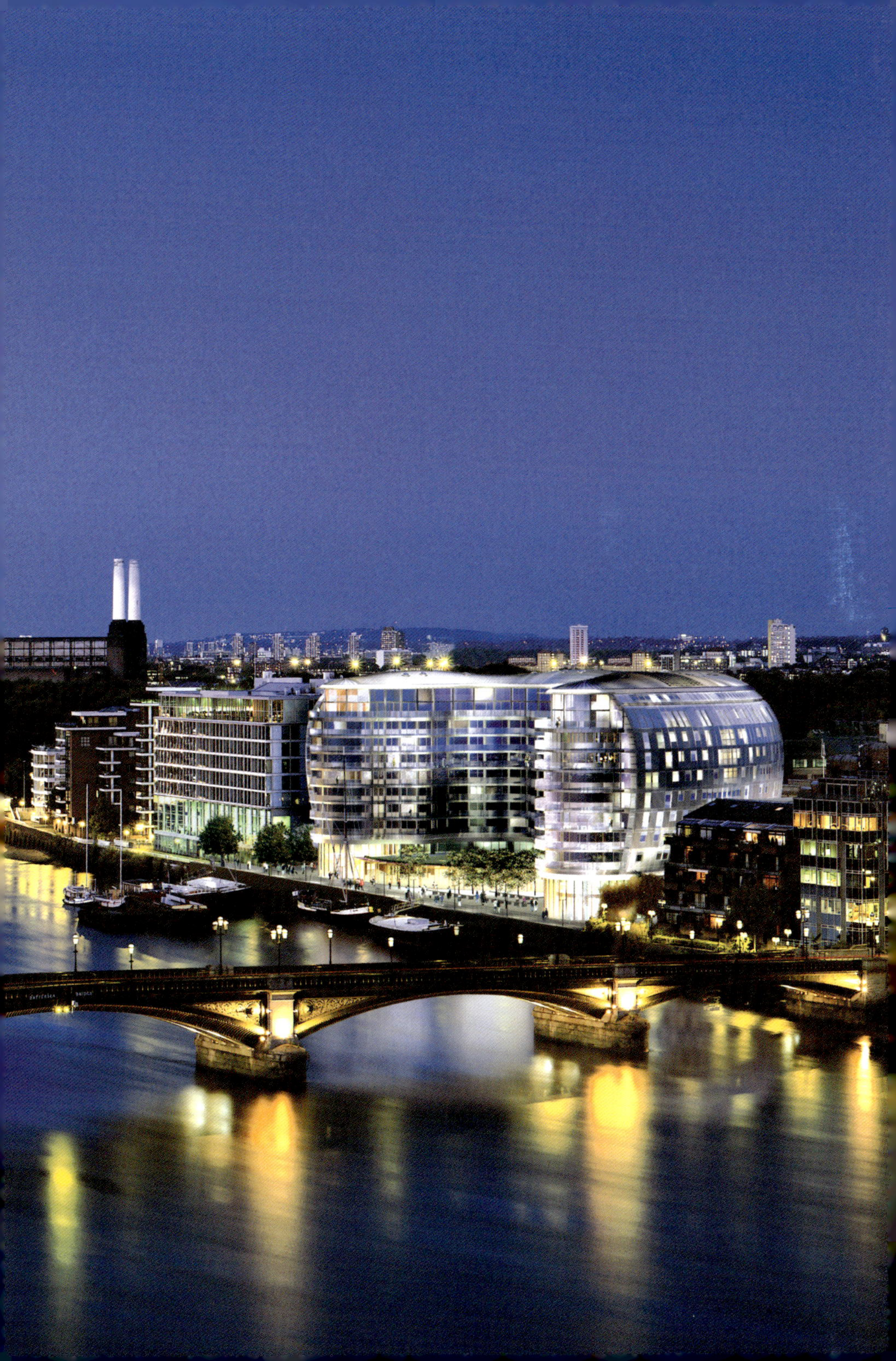

albion RIVERSIDE

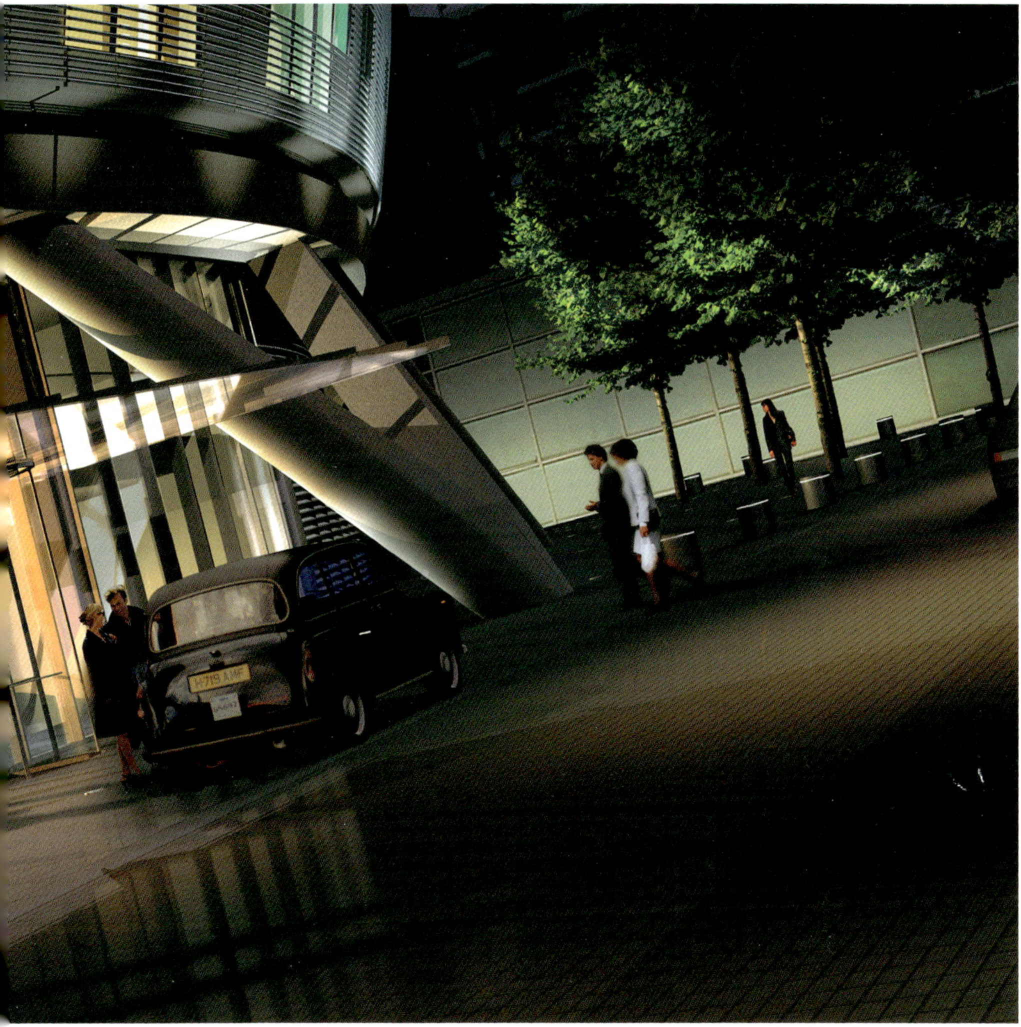

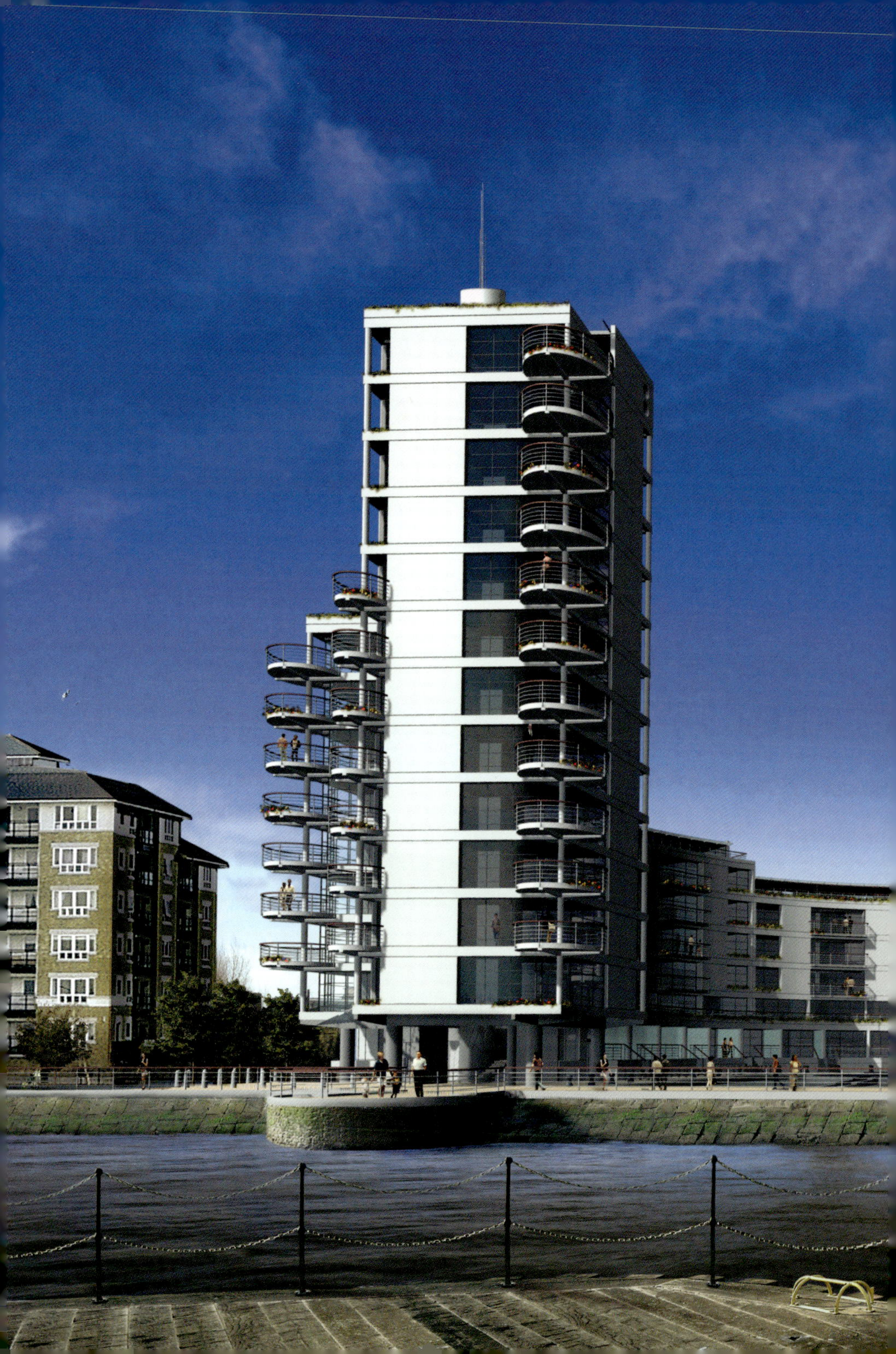

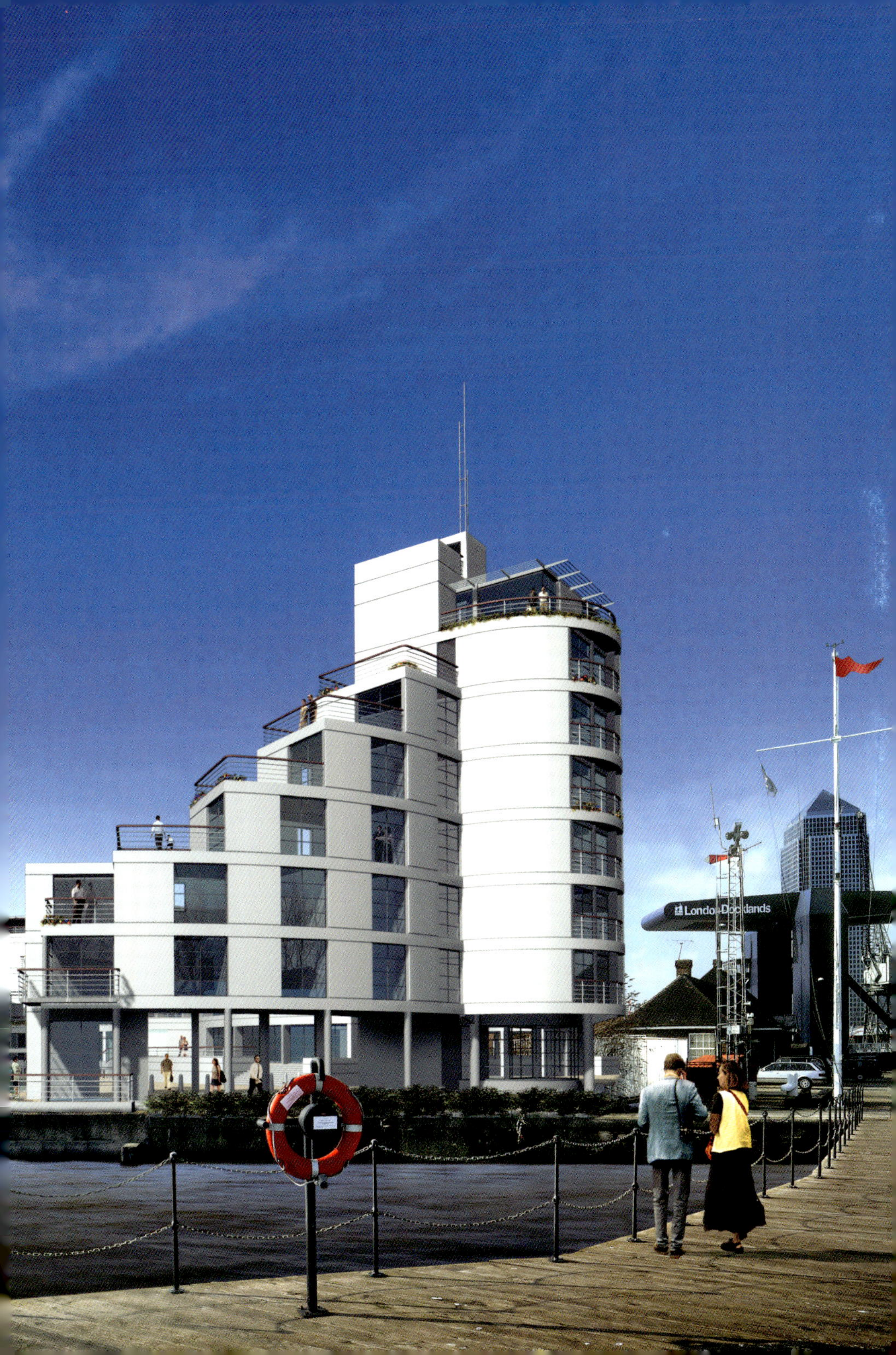
Londo Docklands

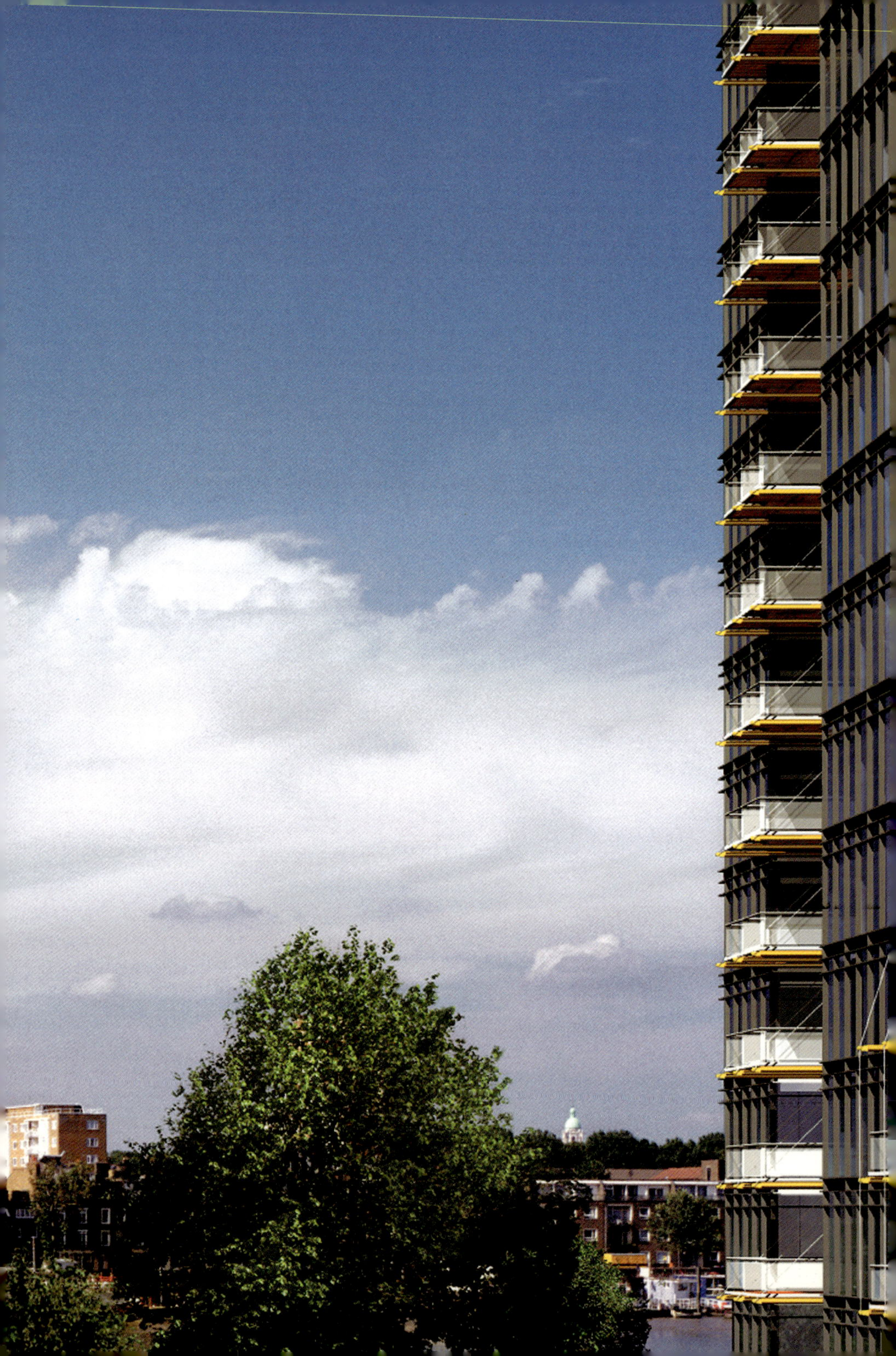

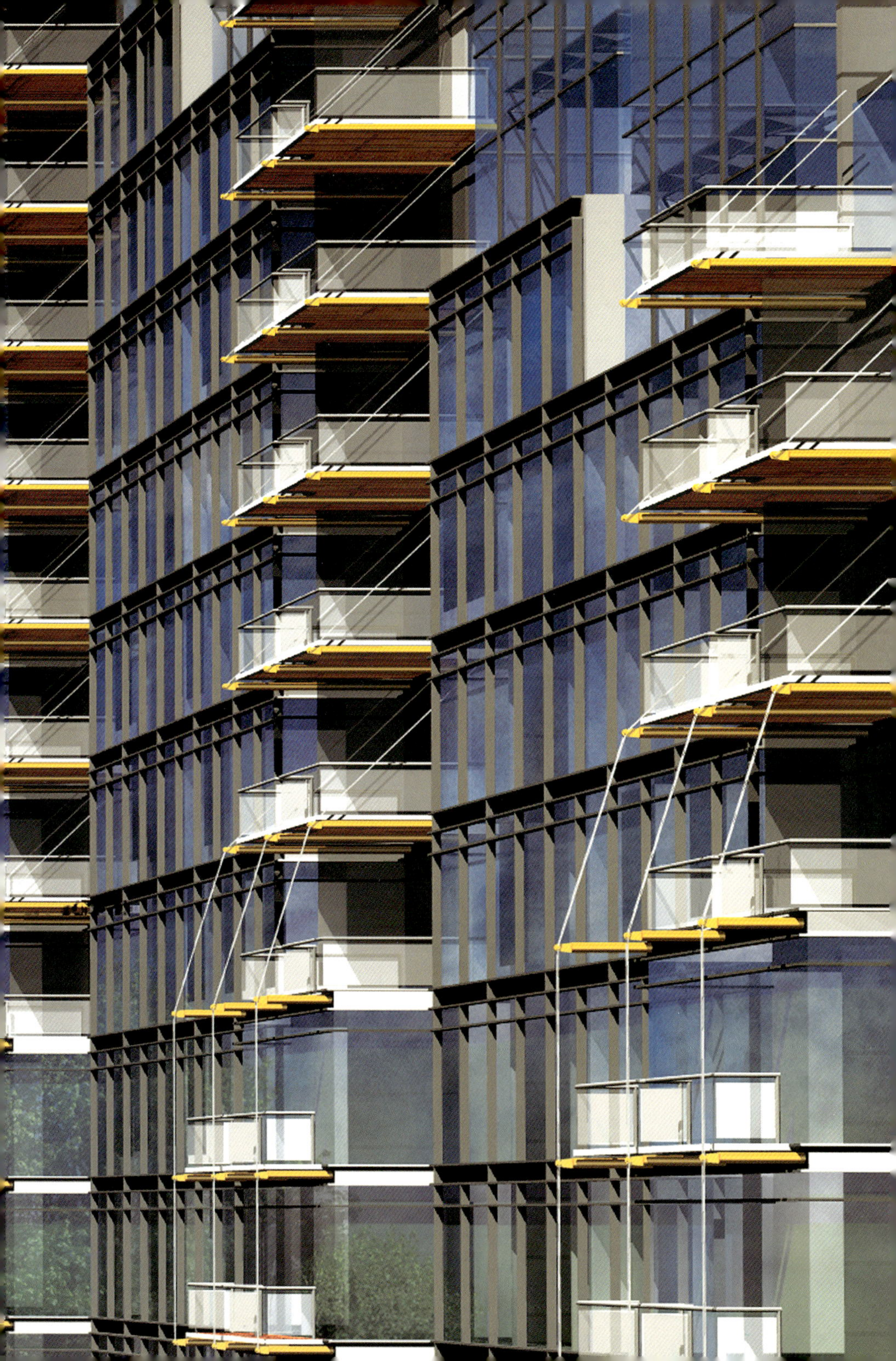

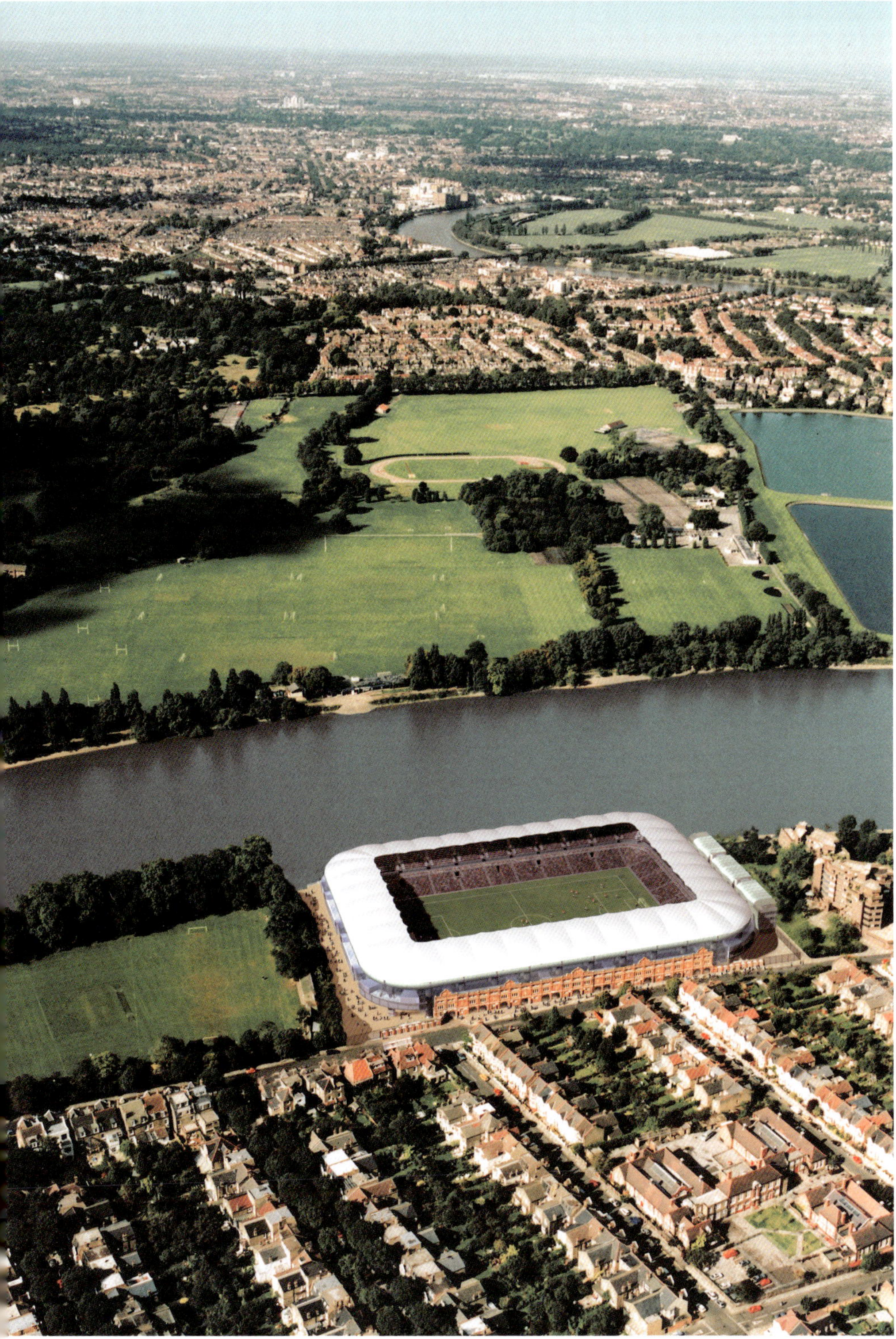

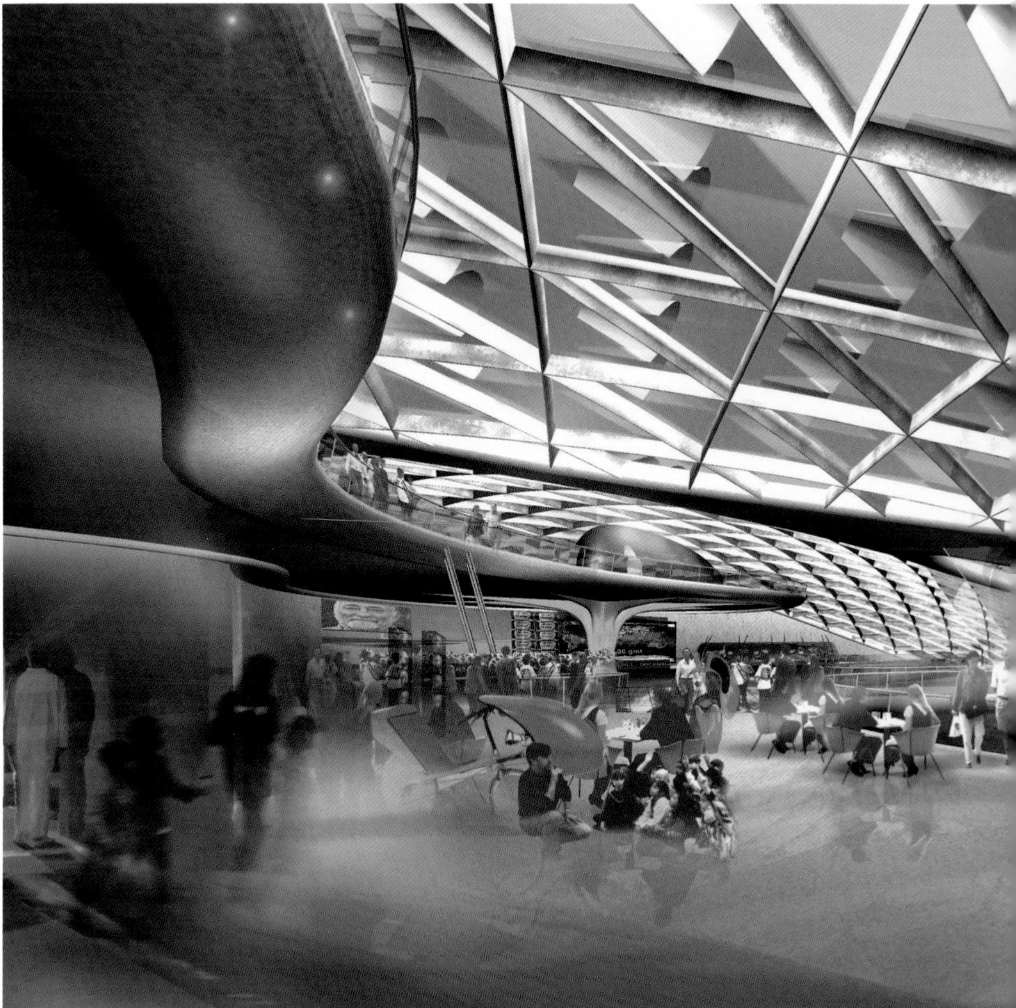

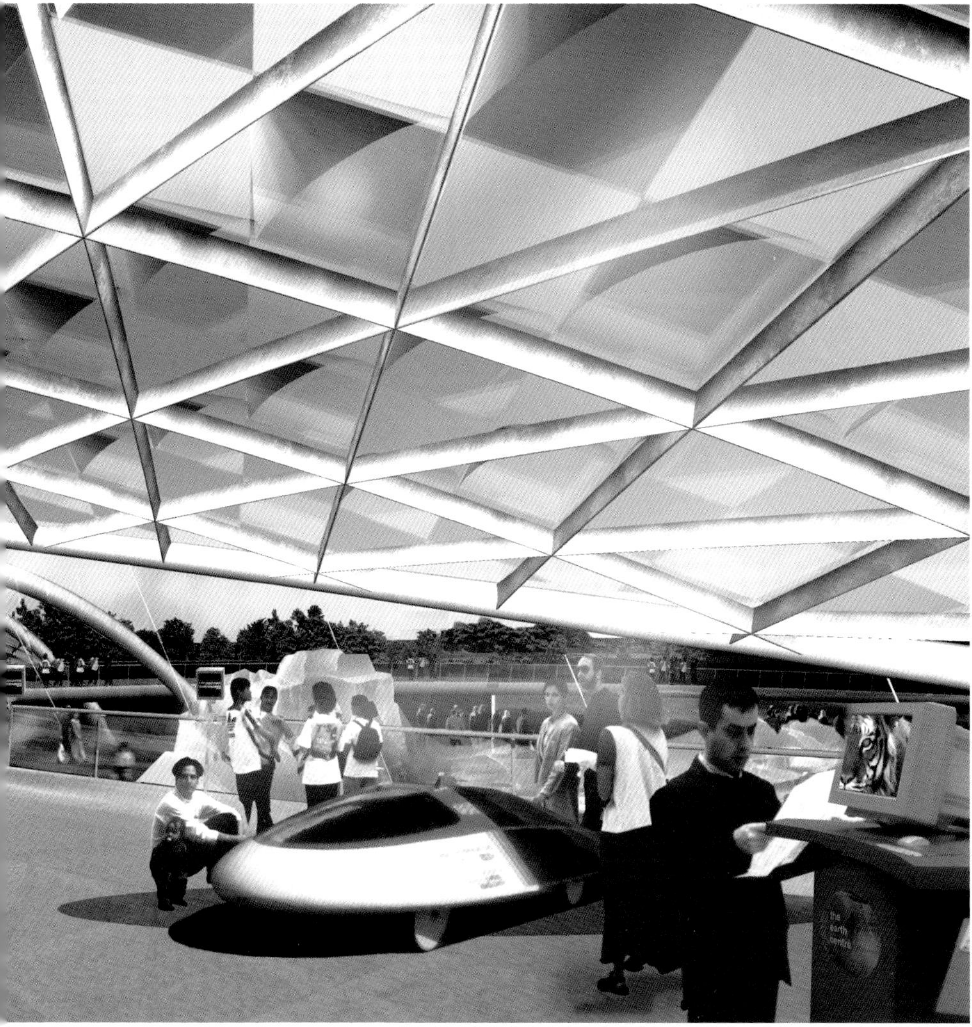

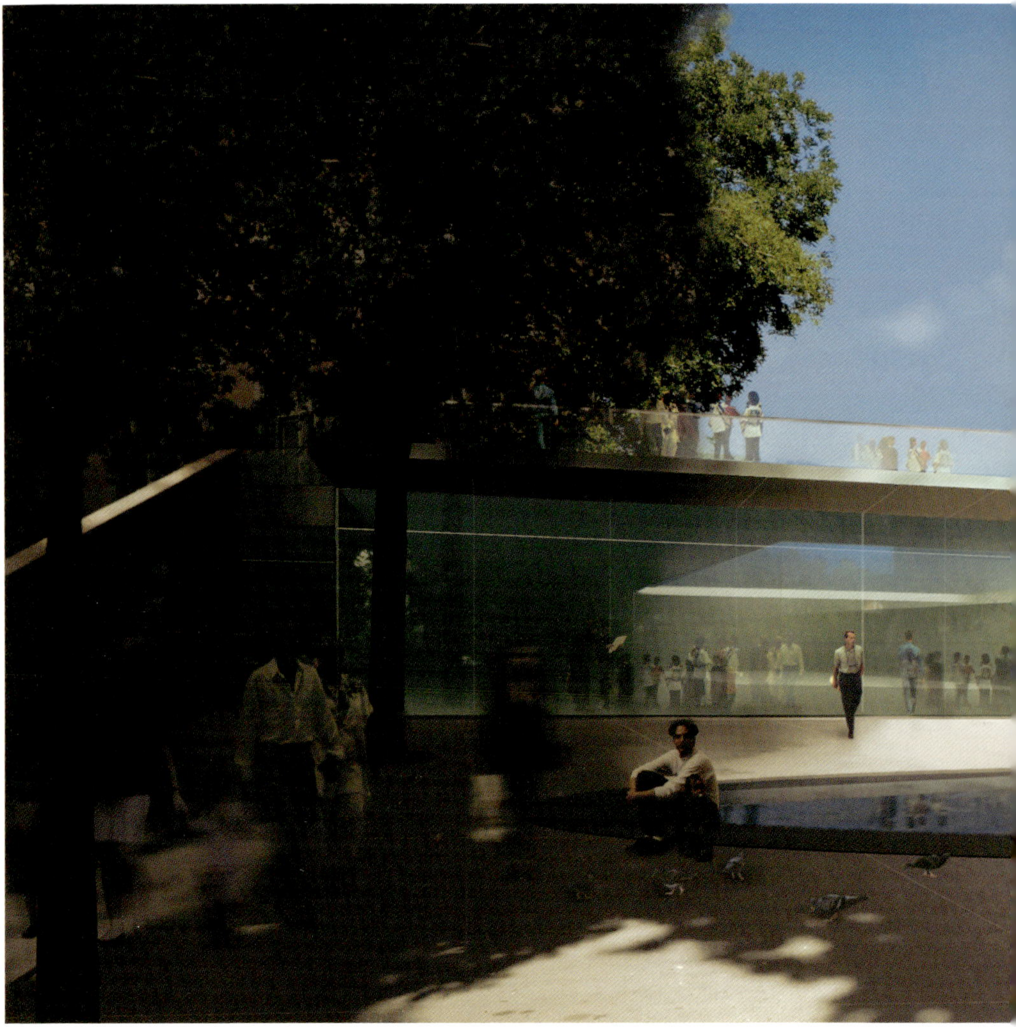

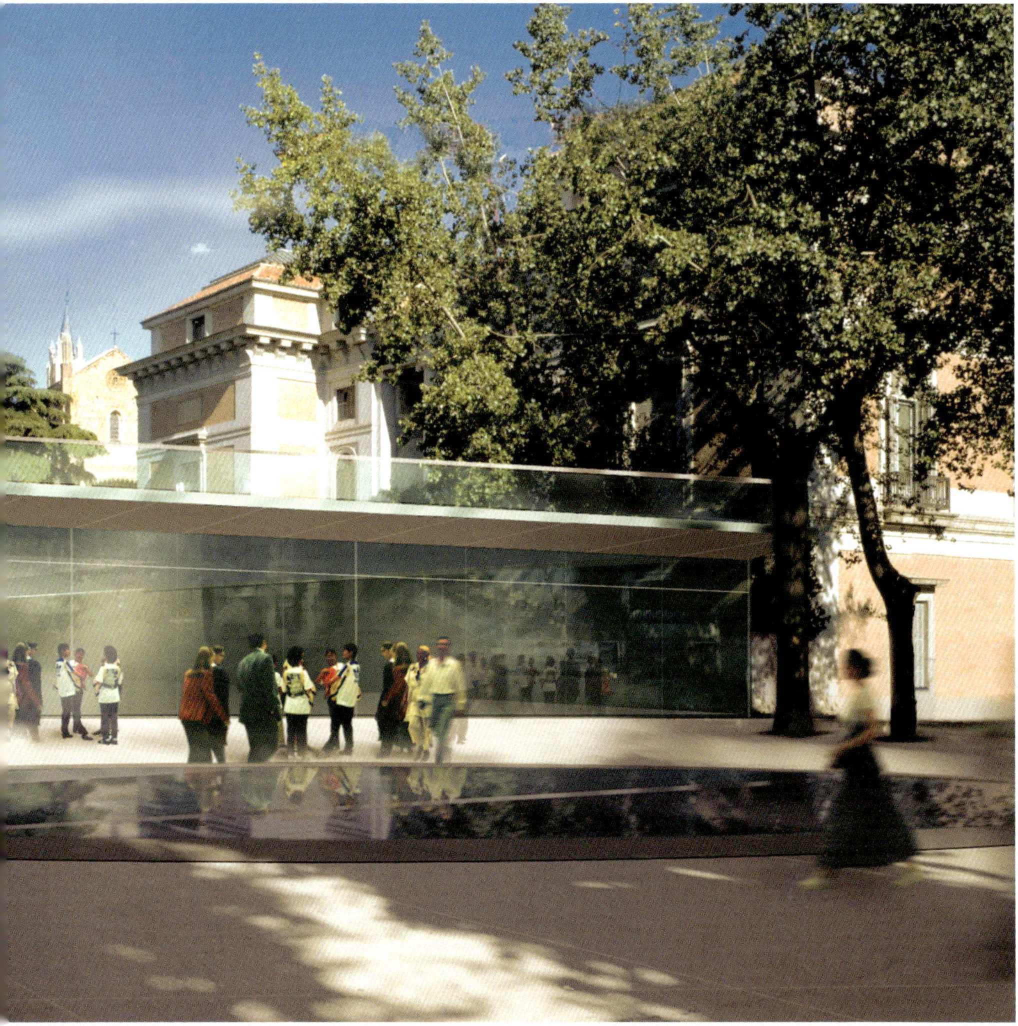

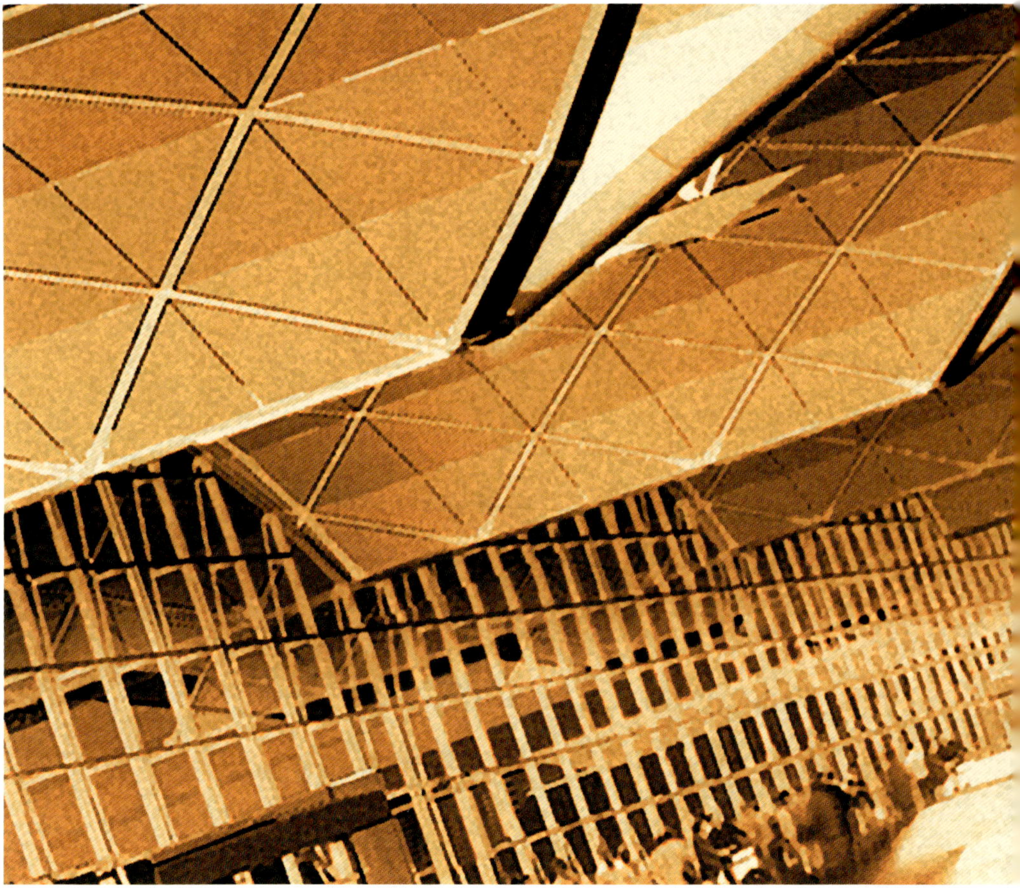

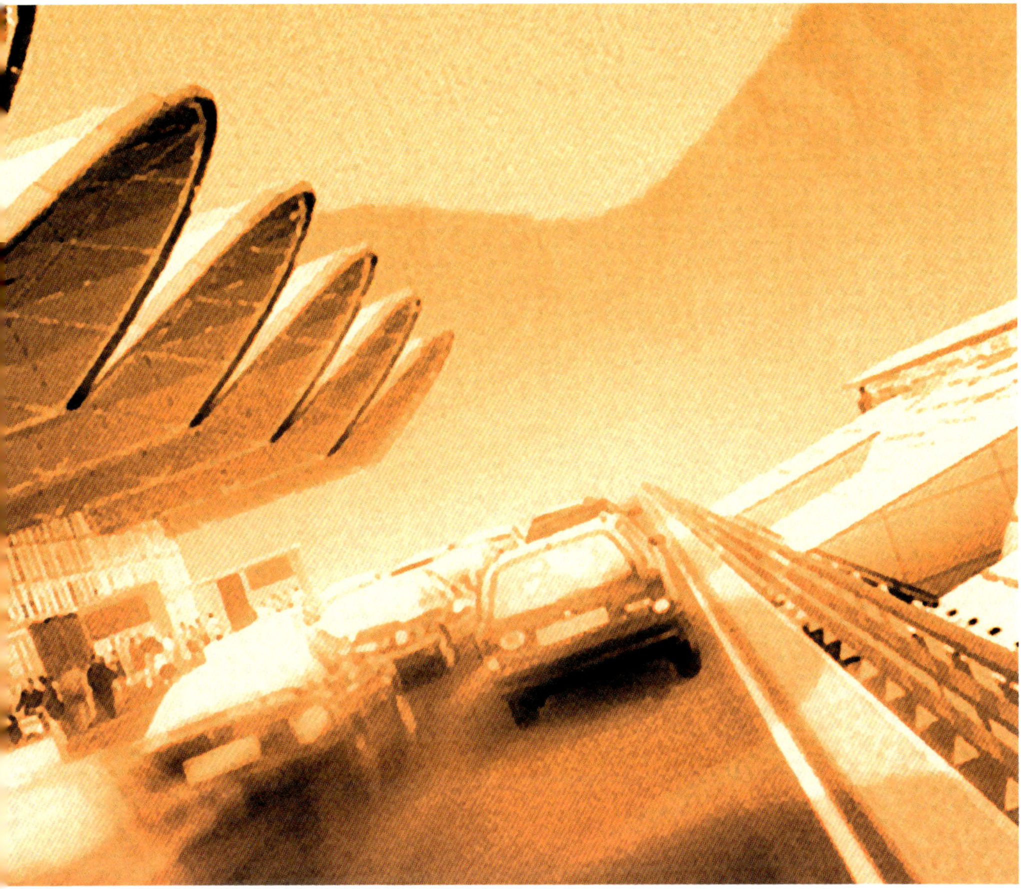

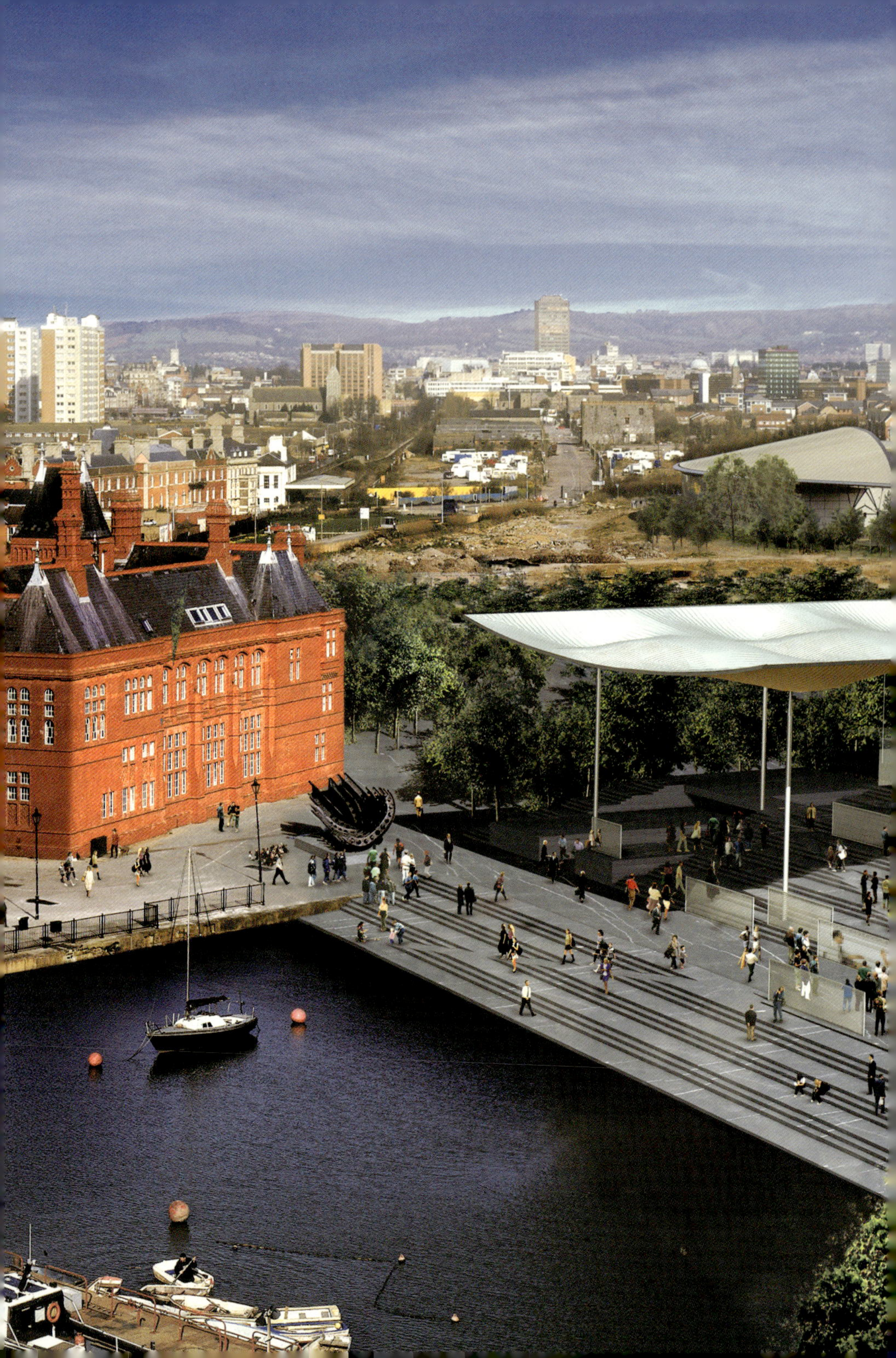

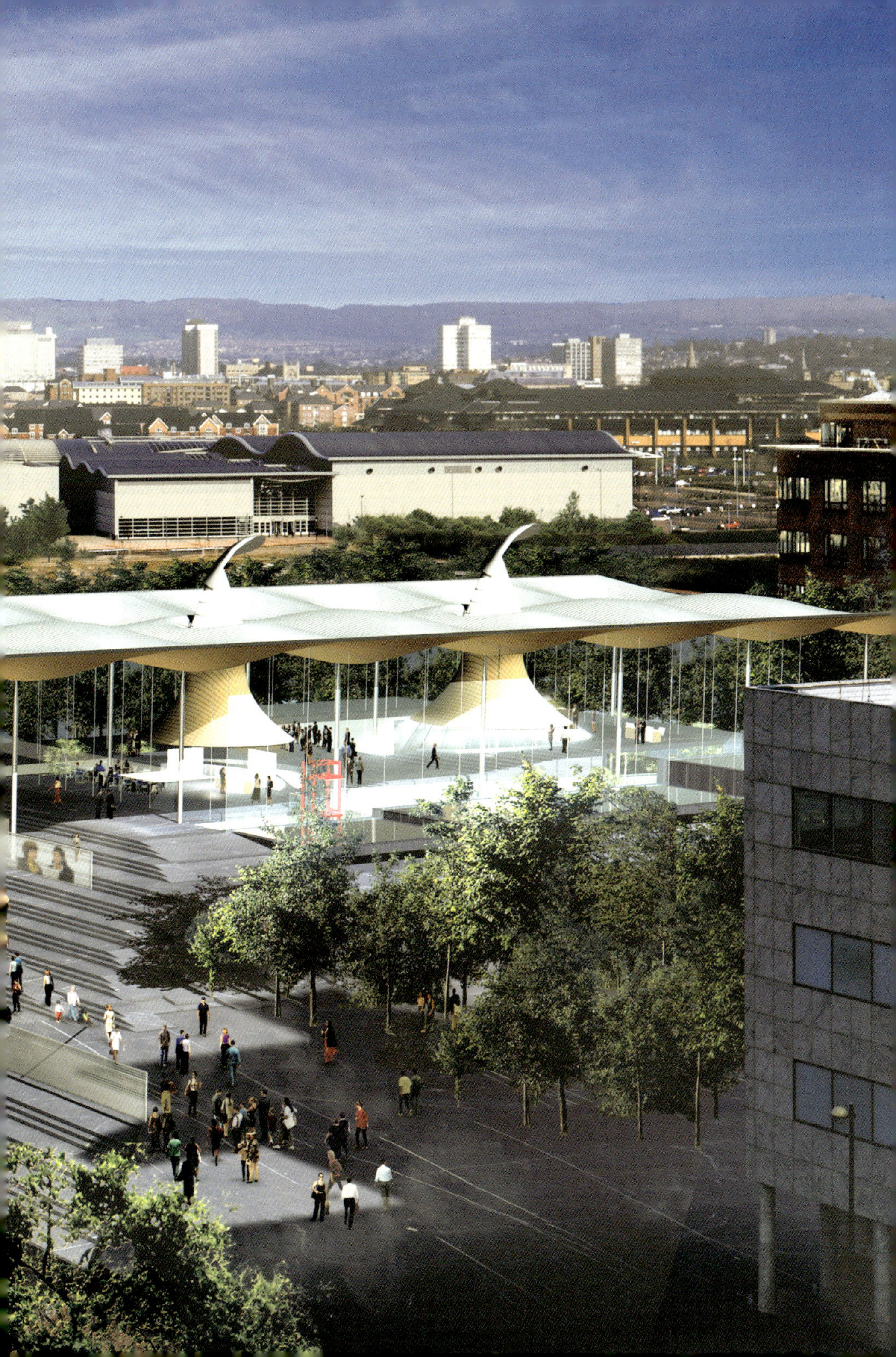

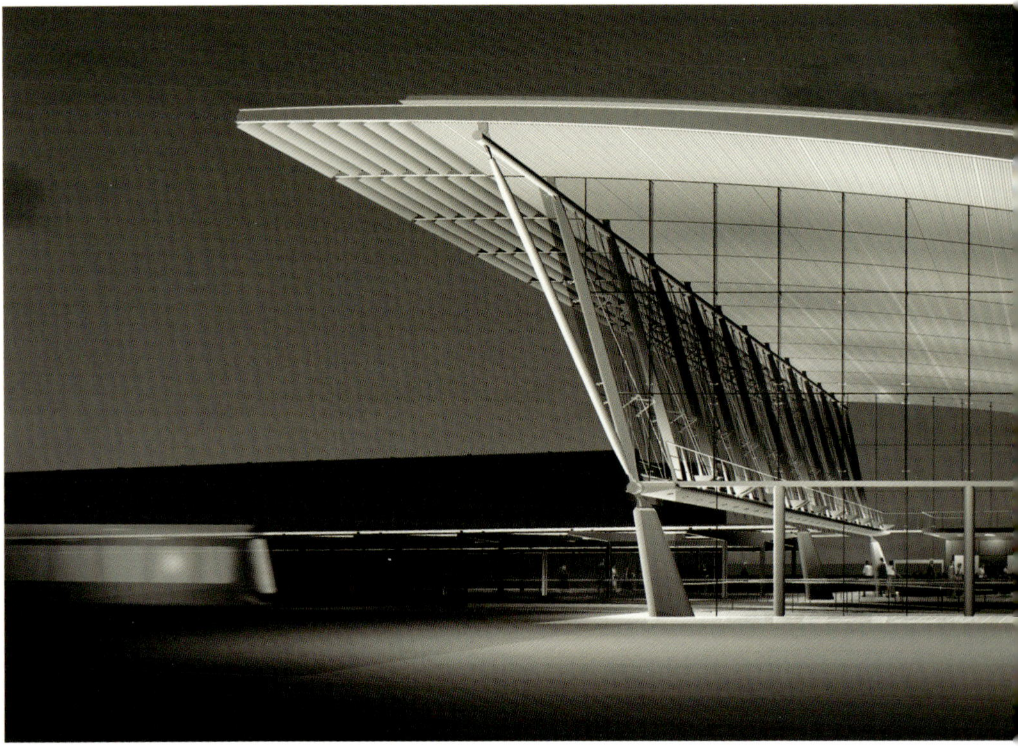

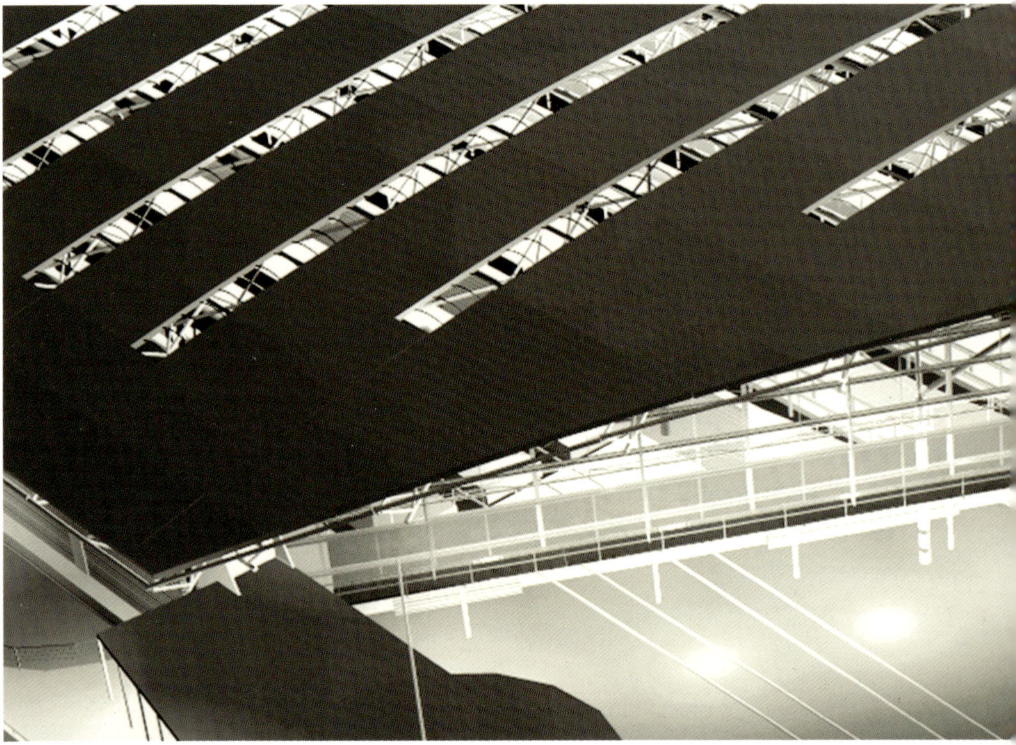

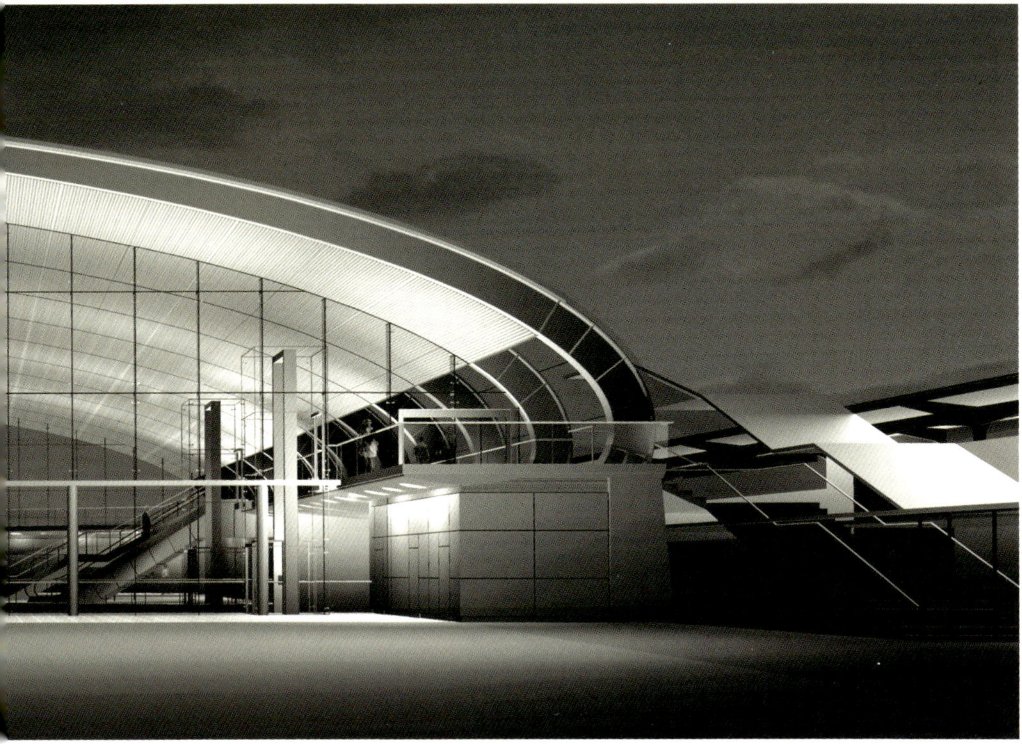

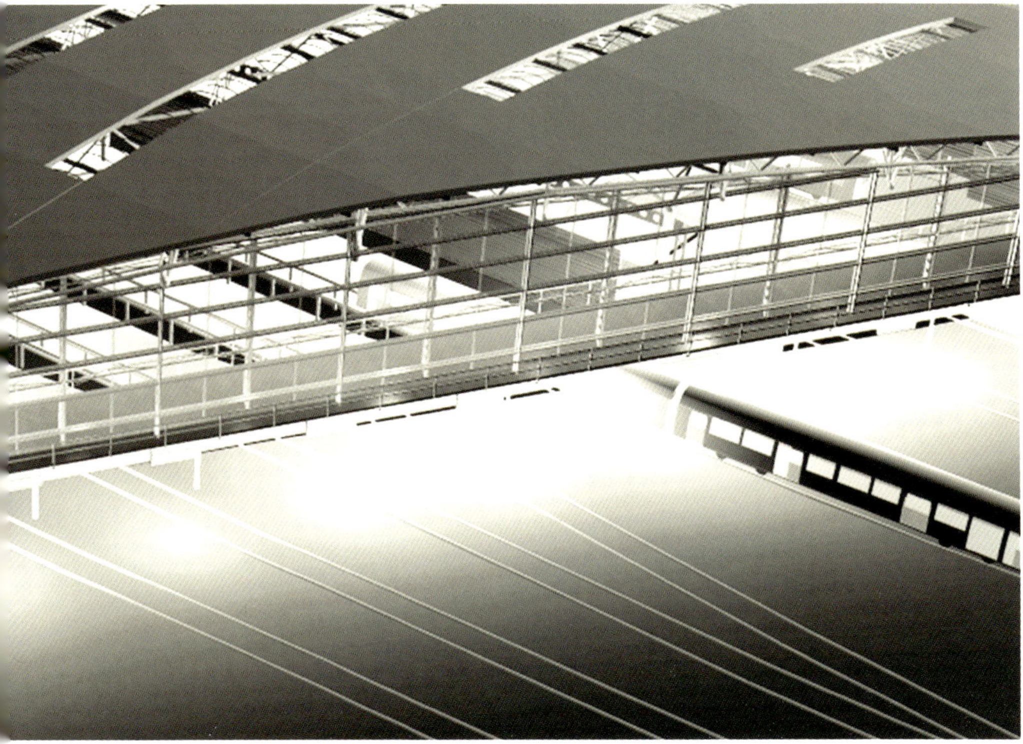

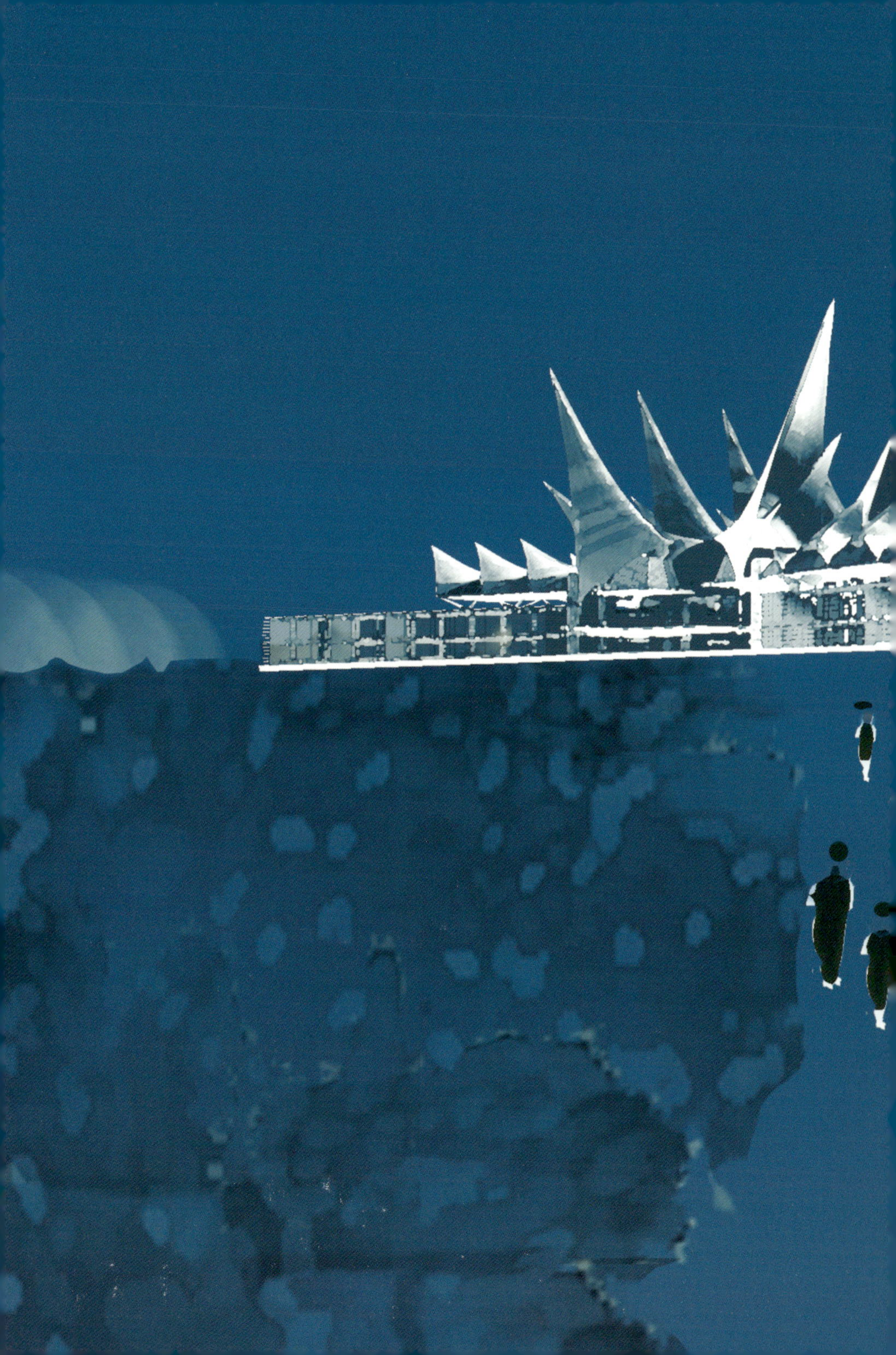

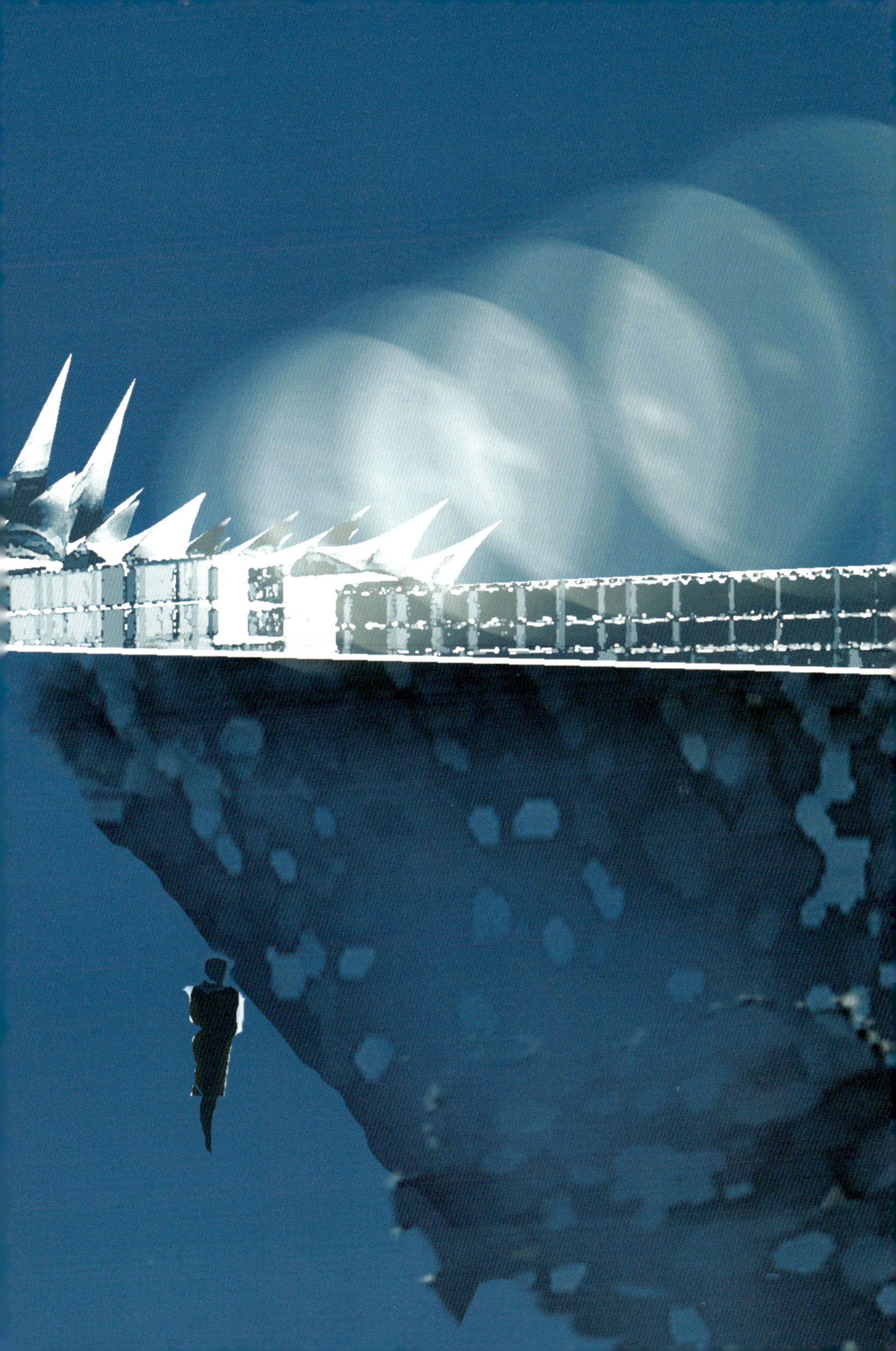

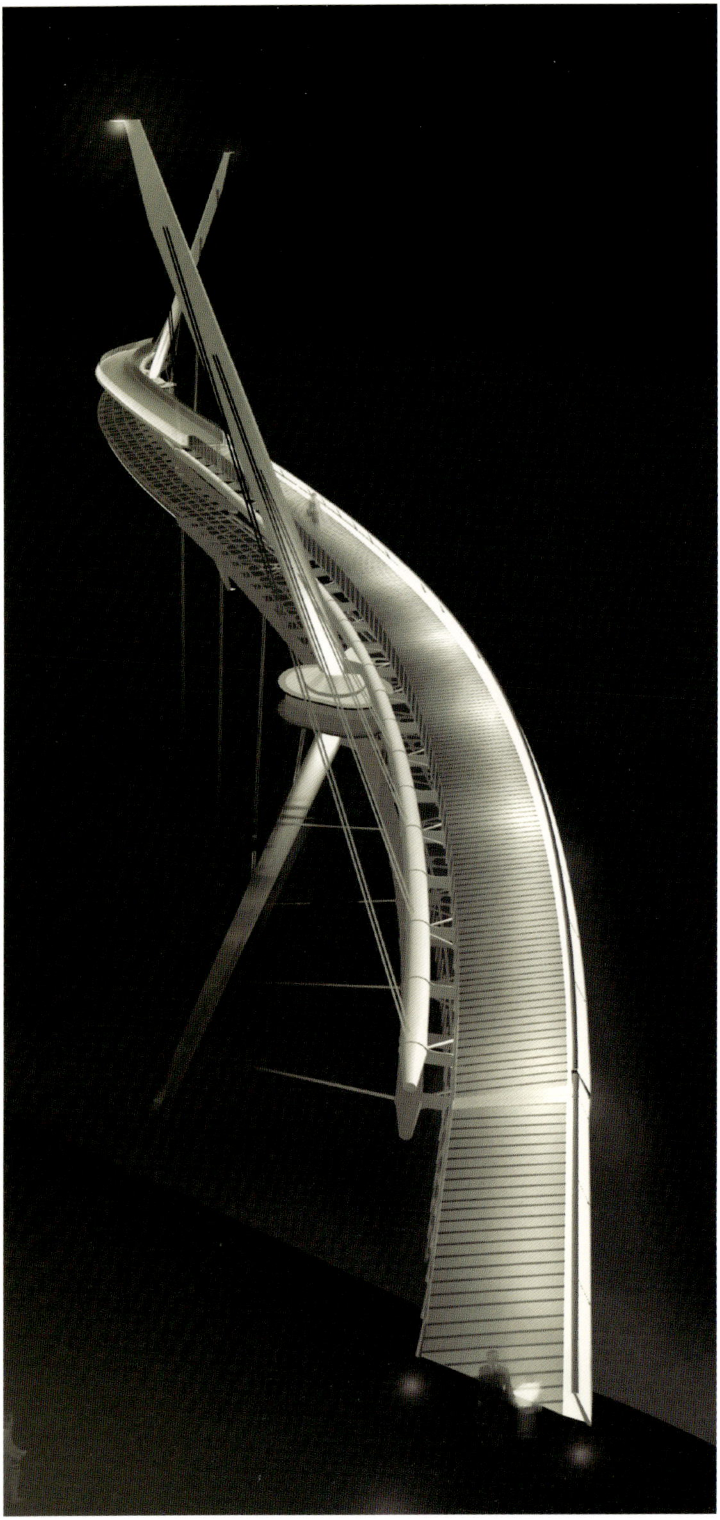

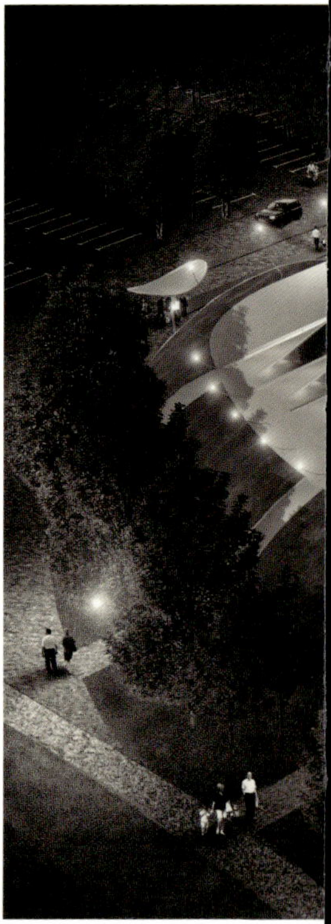

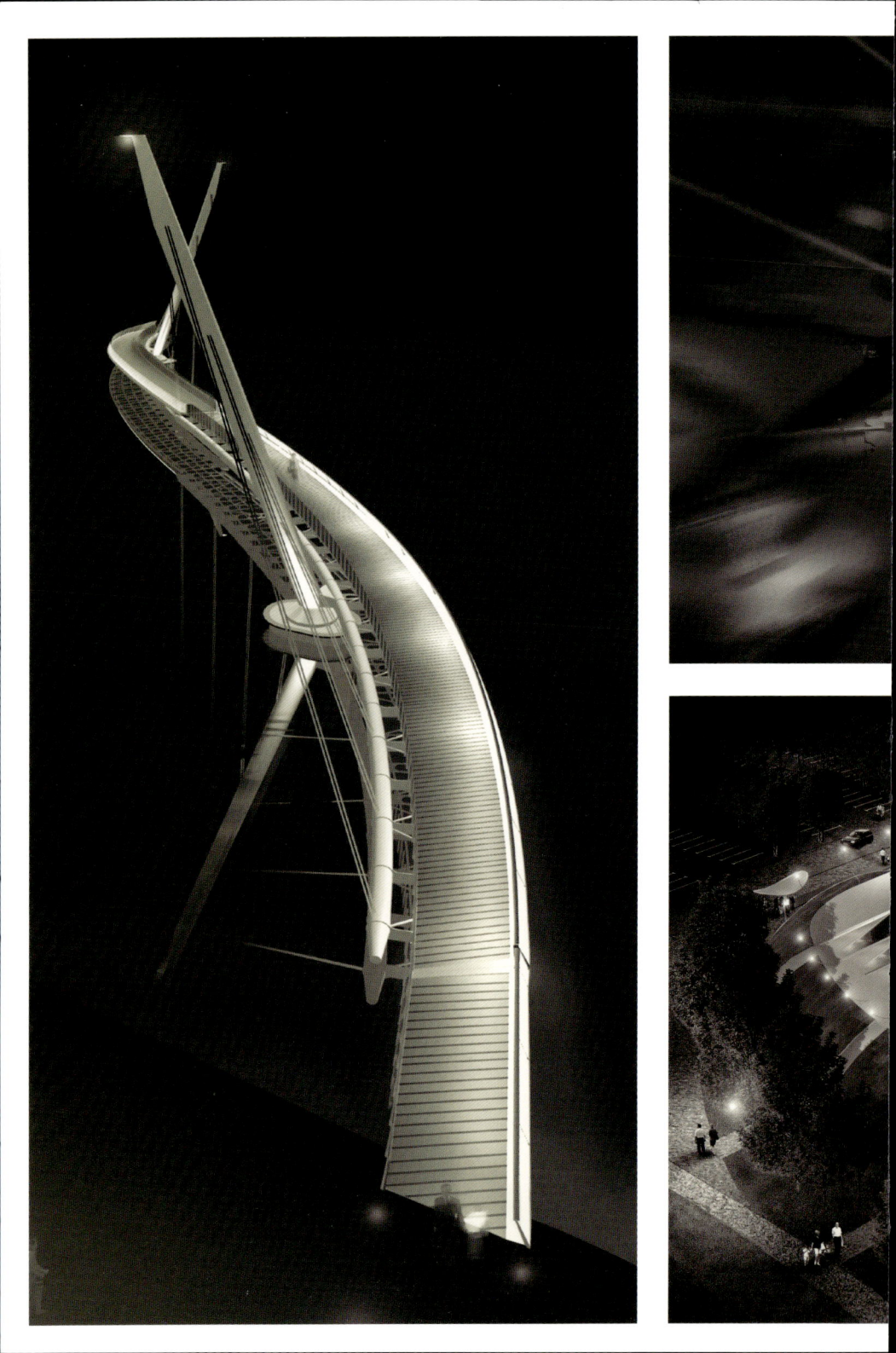

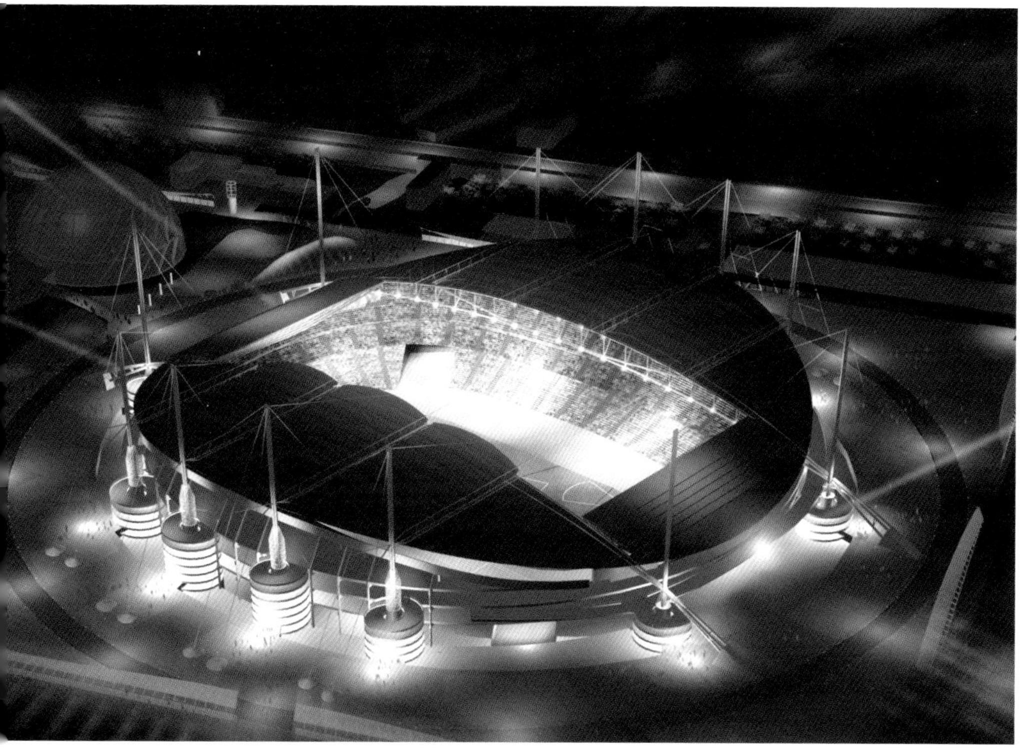

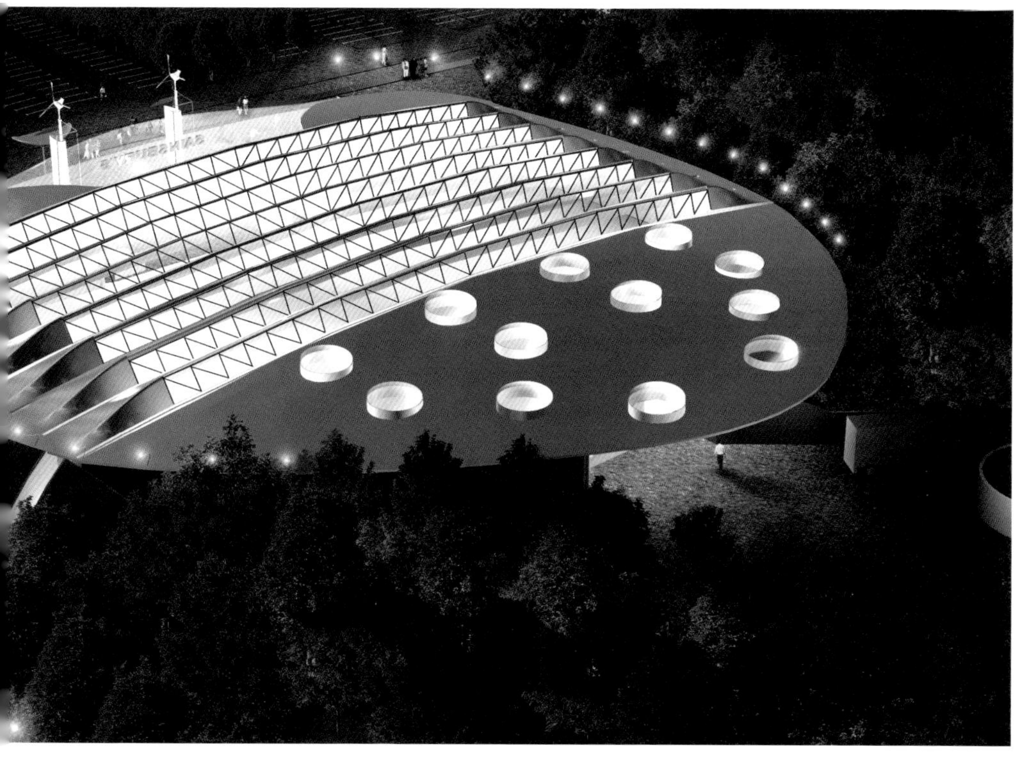

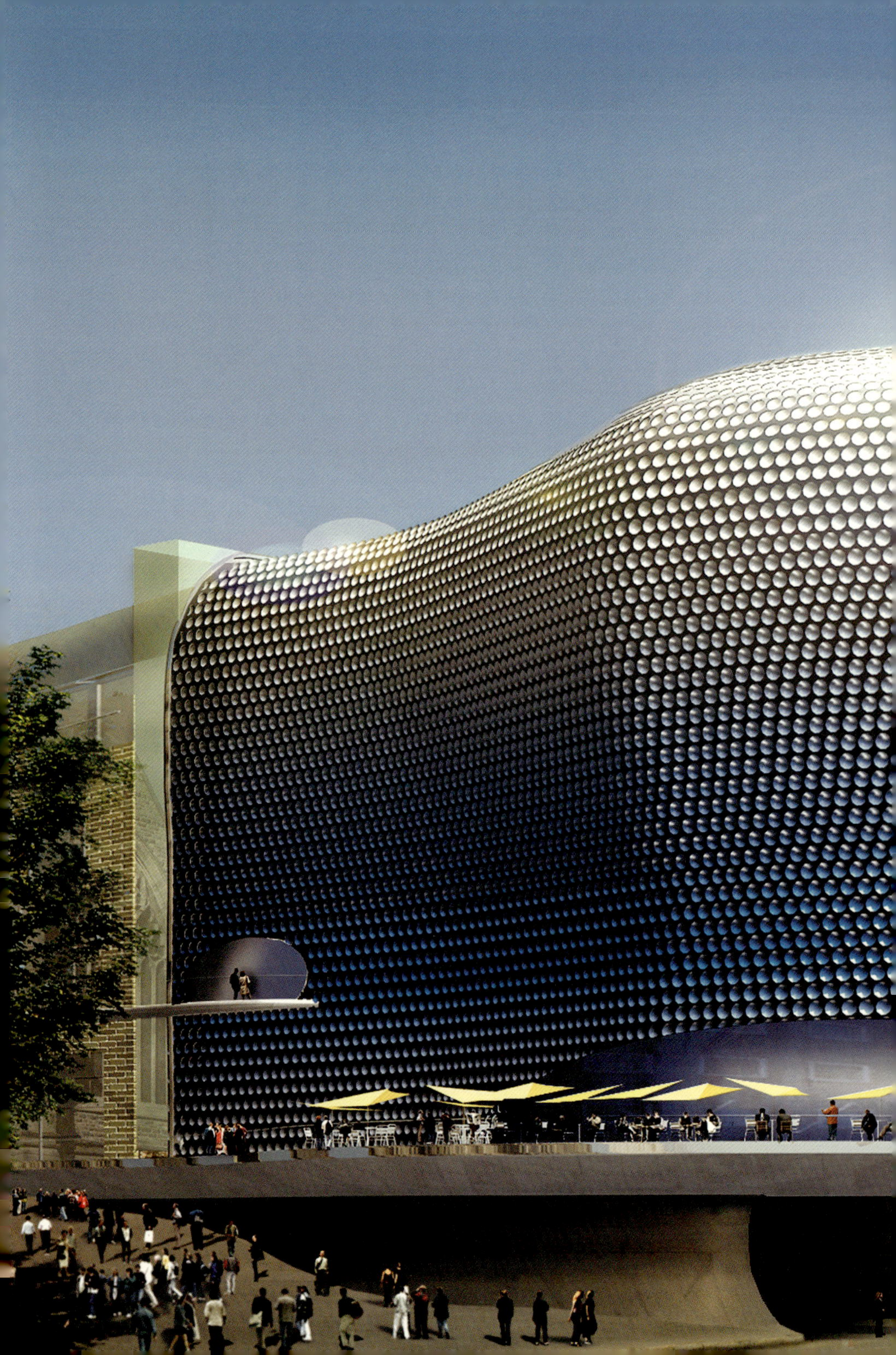

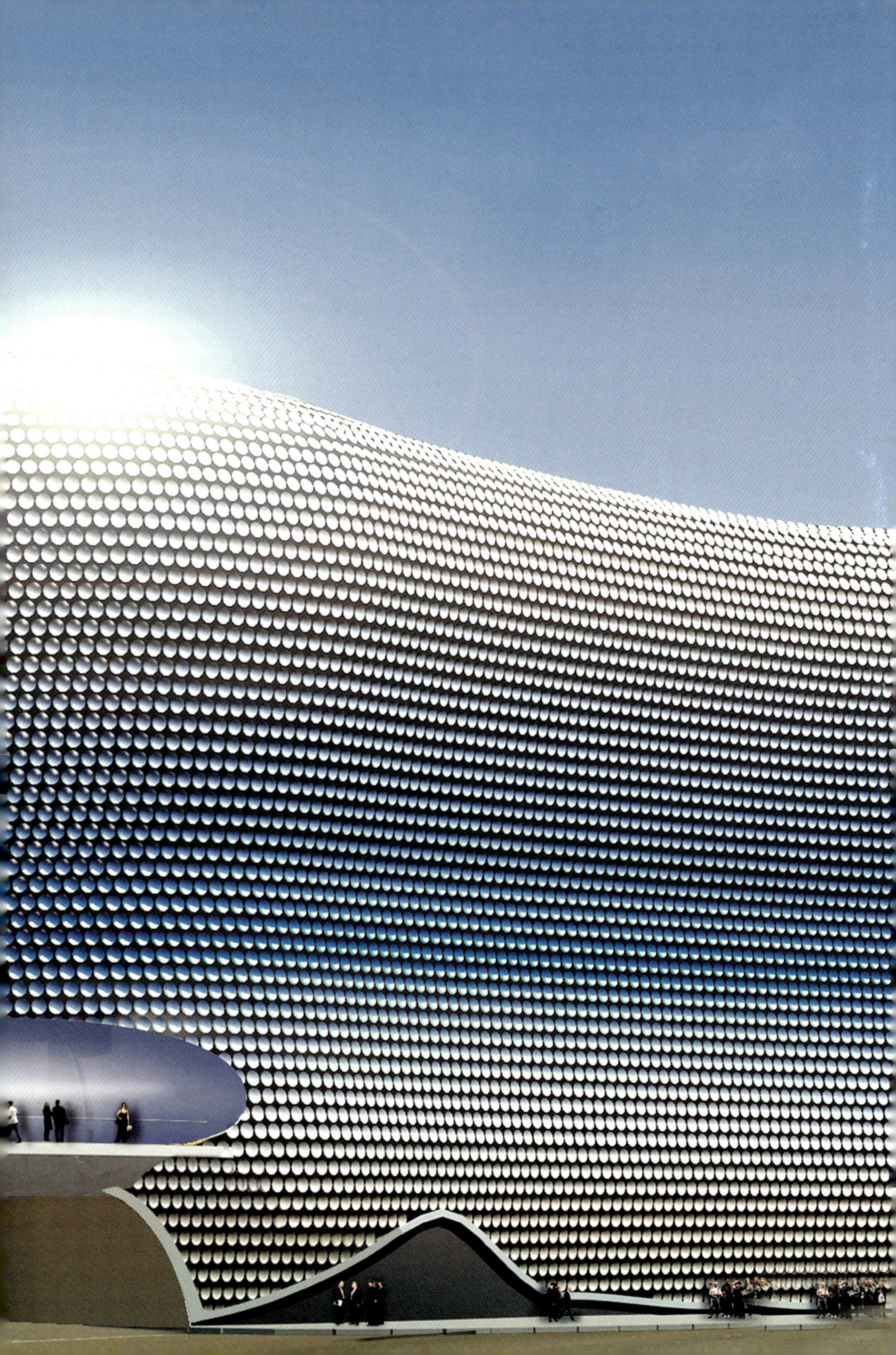

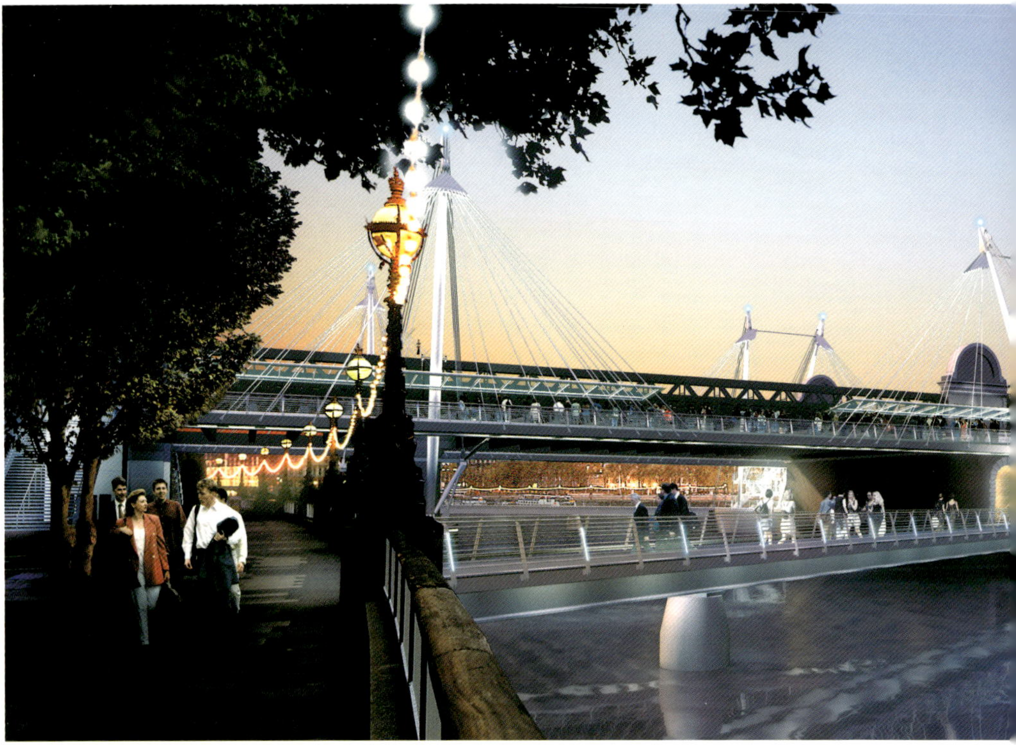

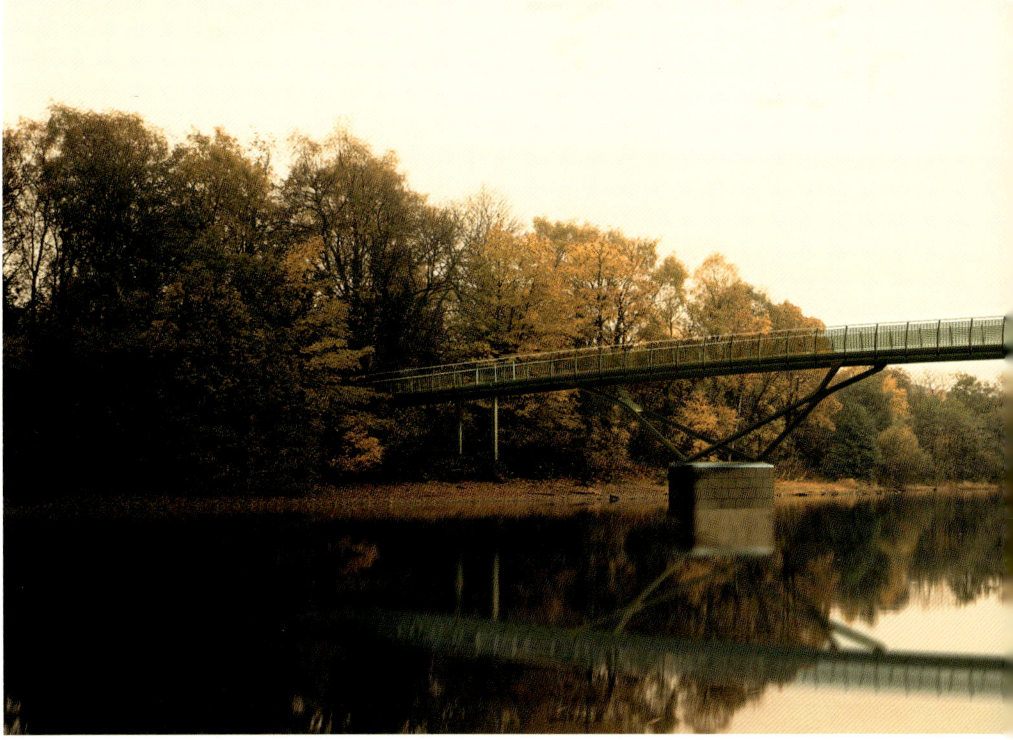

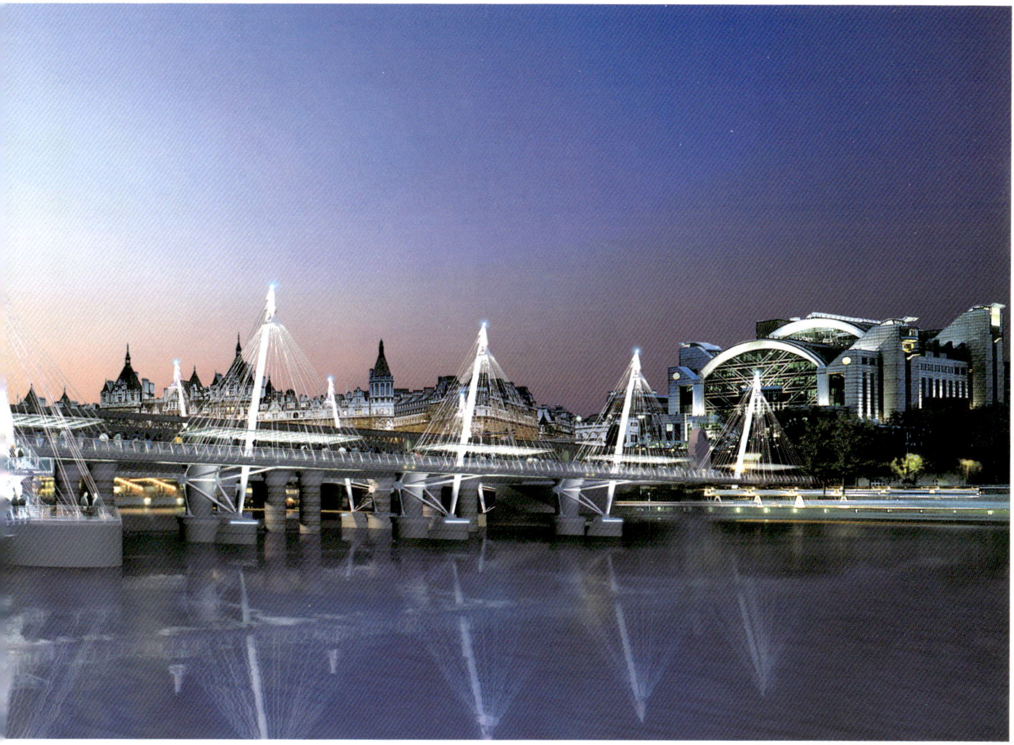

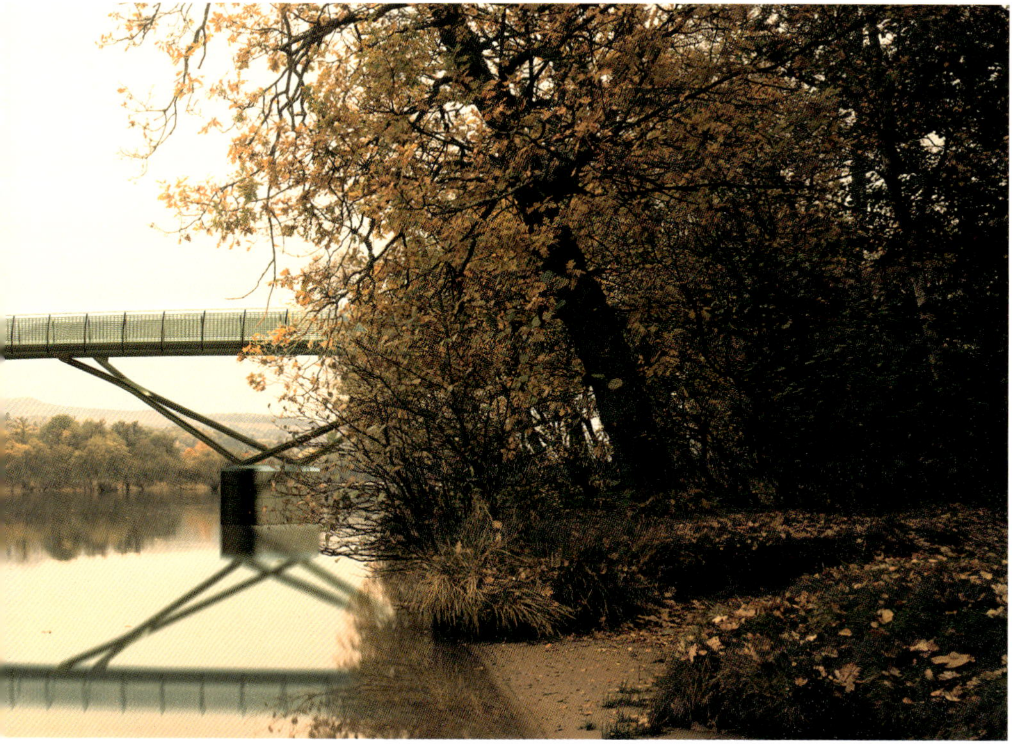

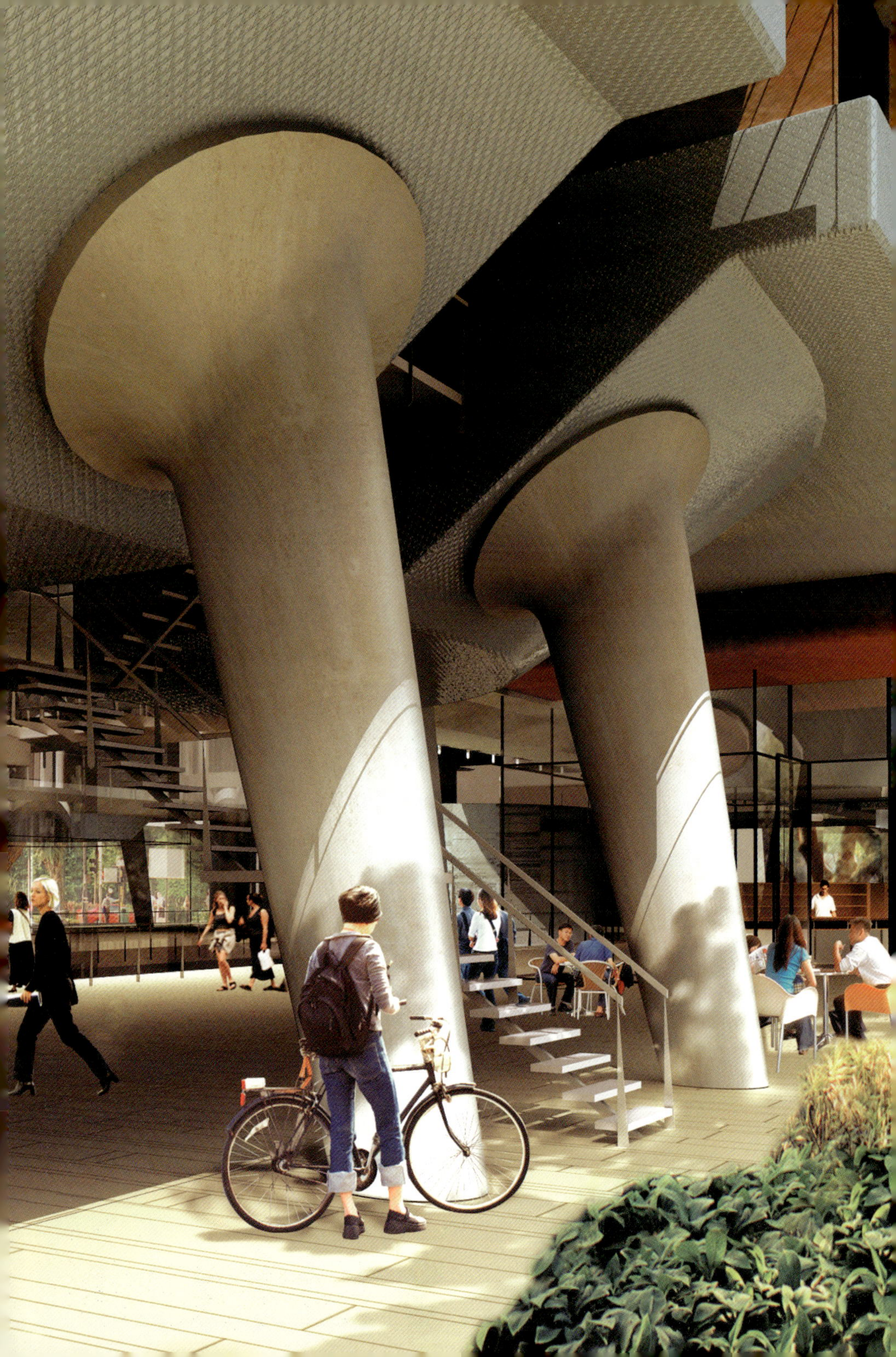

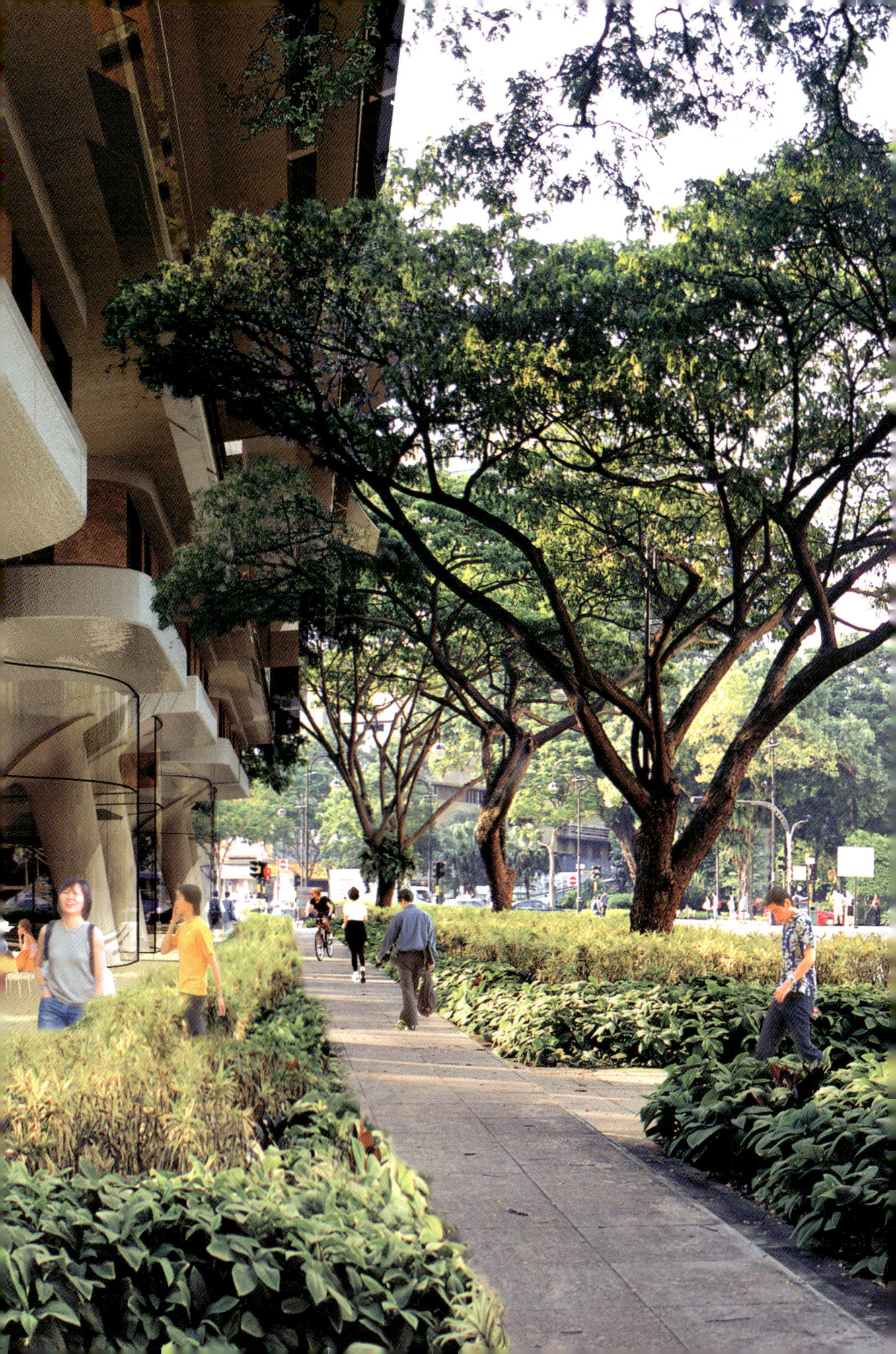

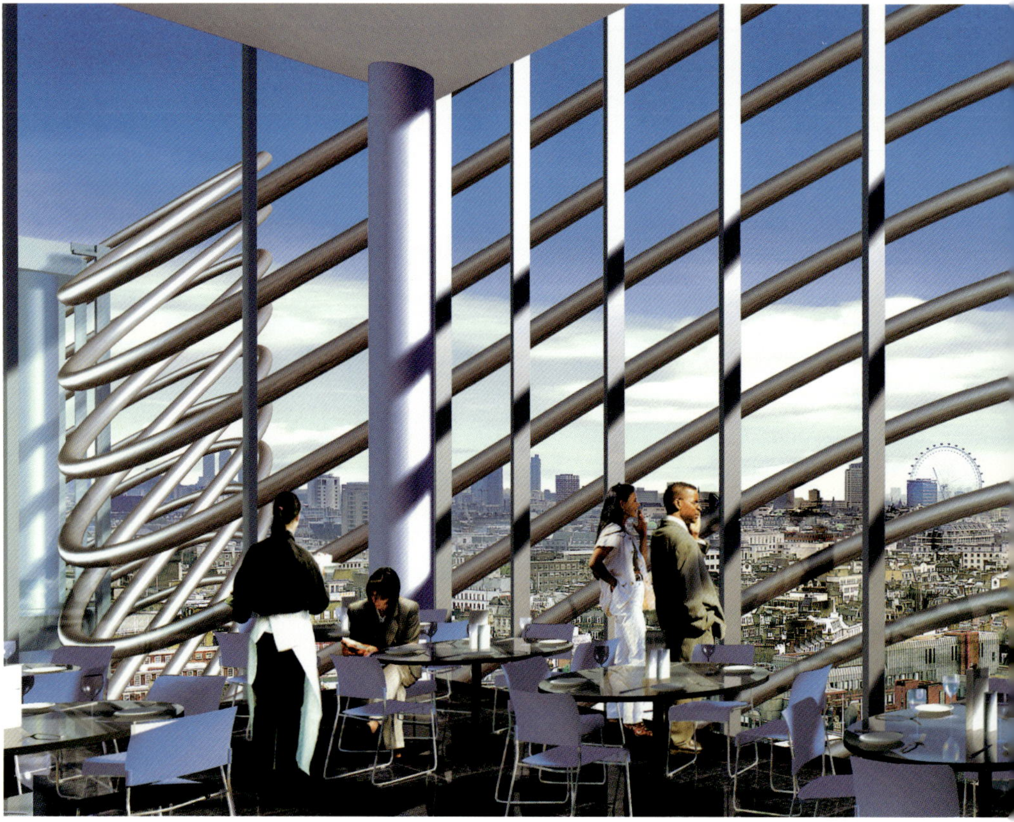

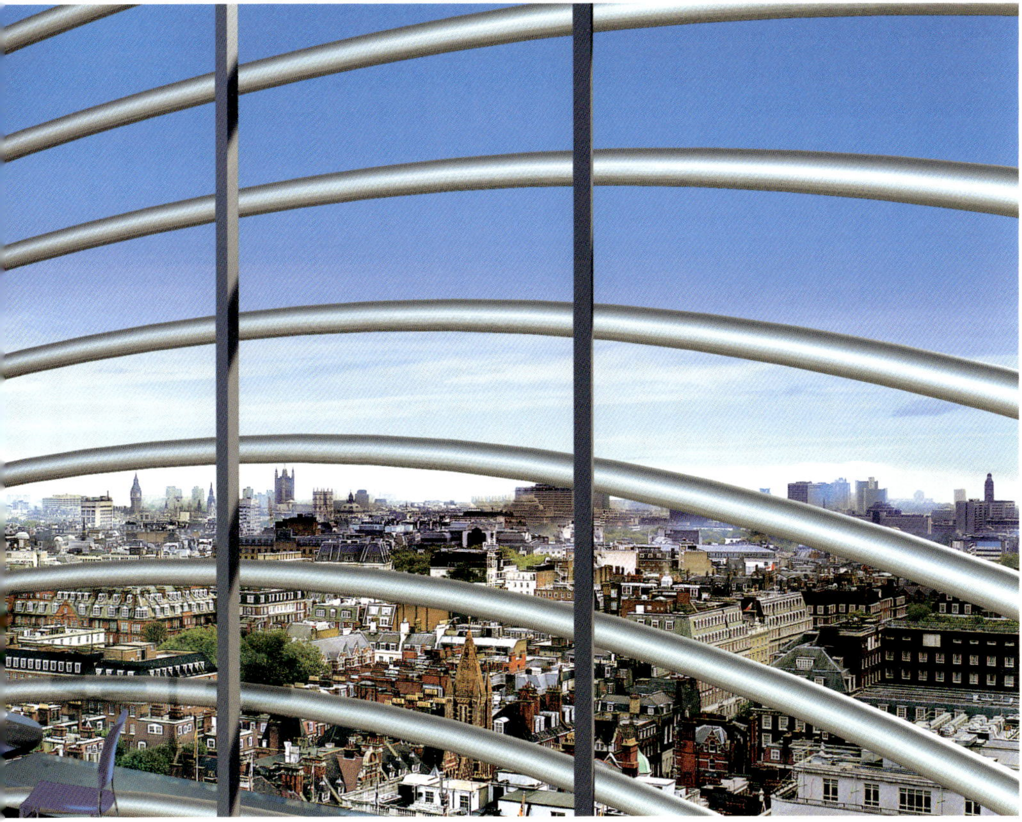

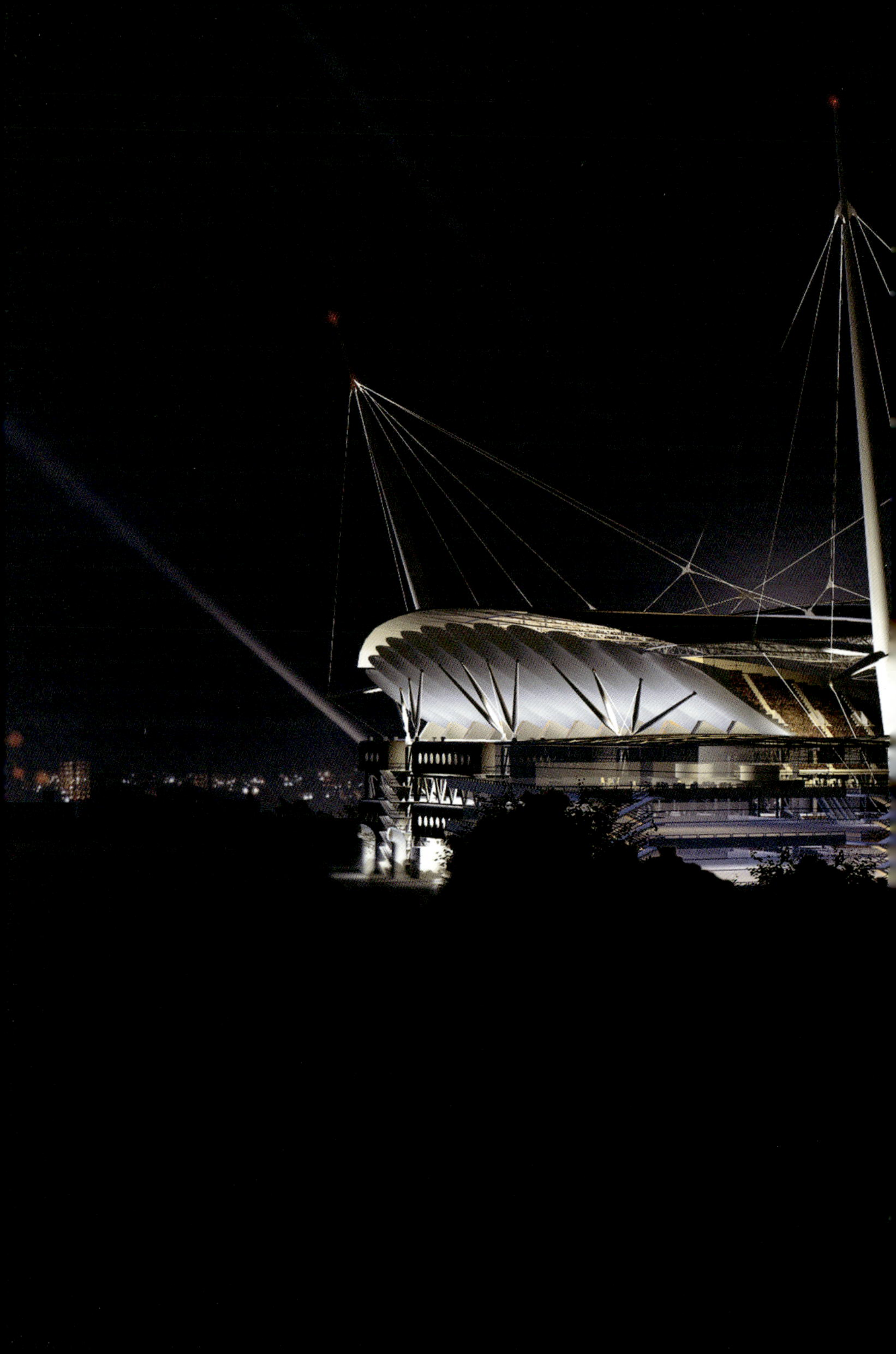

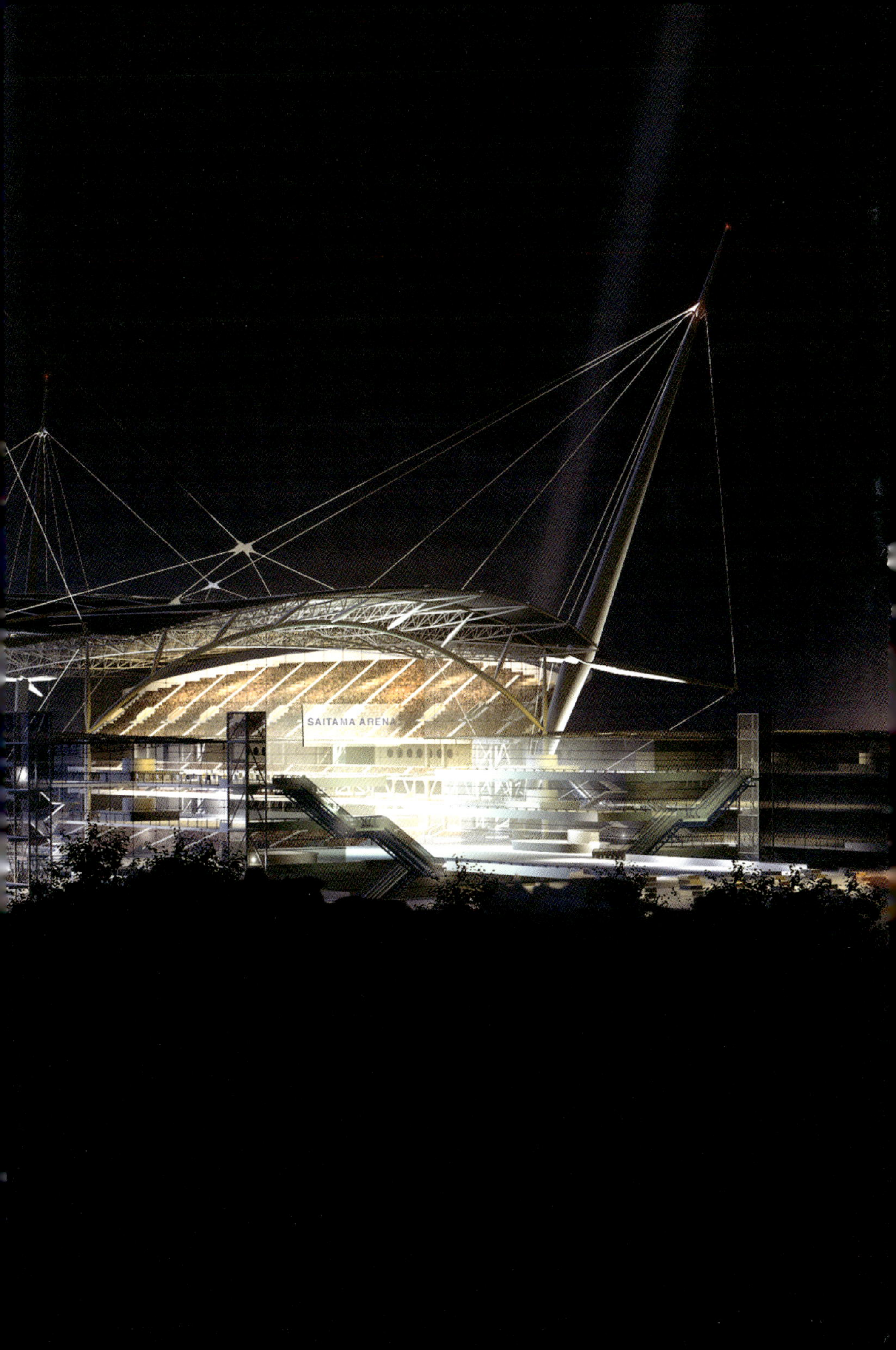
SAITAMA ARENA

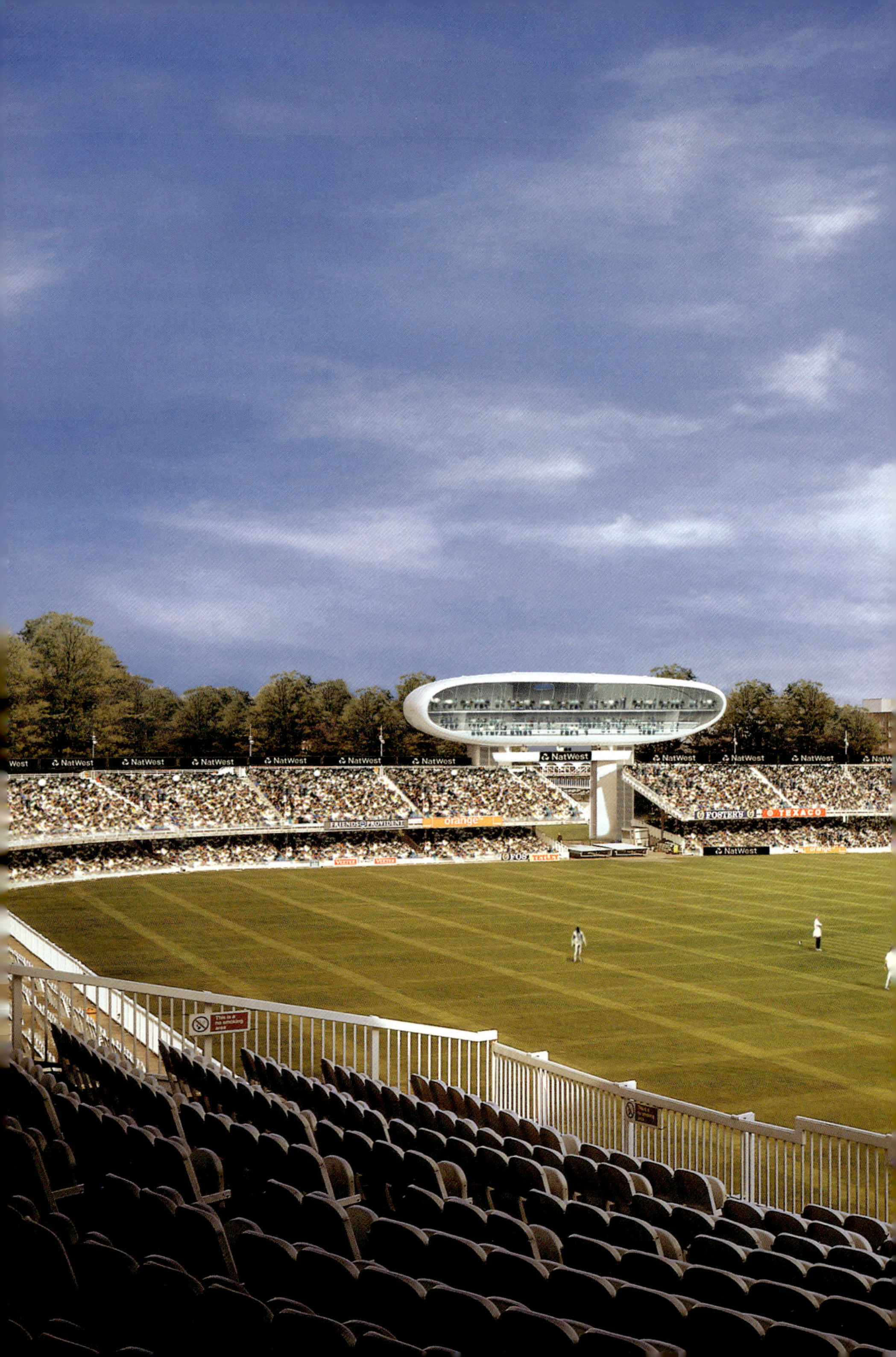
NatWest
FRIENDS PROVIDENT
orange
FOSTER'S
TEXACO

NatWest
WEETABIX
FOSTER'S
FOSTER'S
TEXACO
orange
orange
WEETABIX

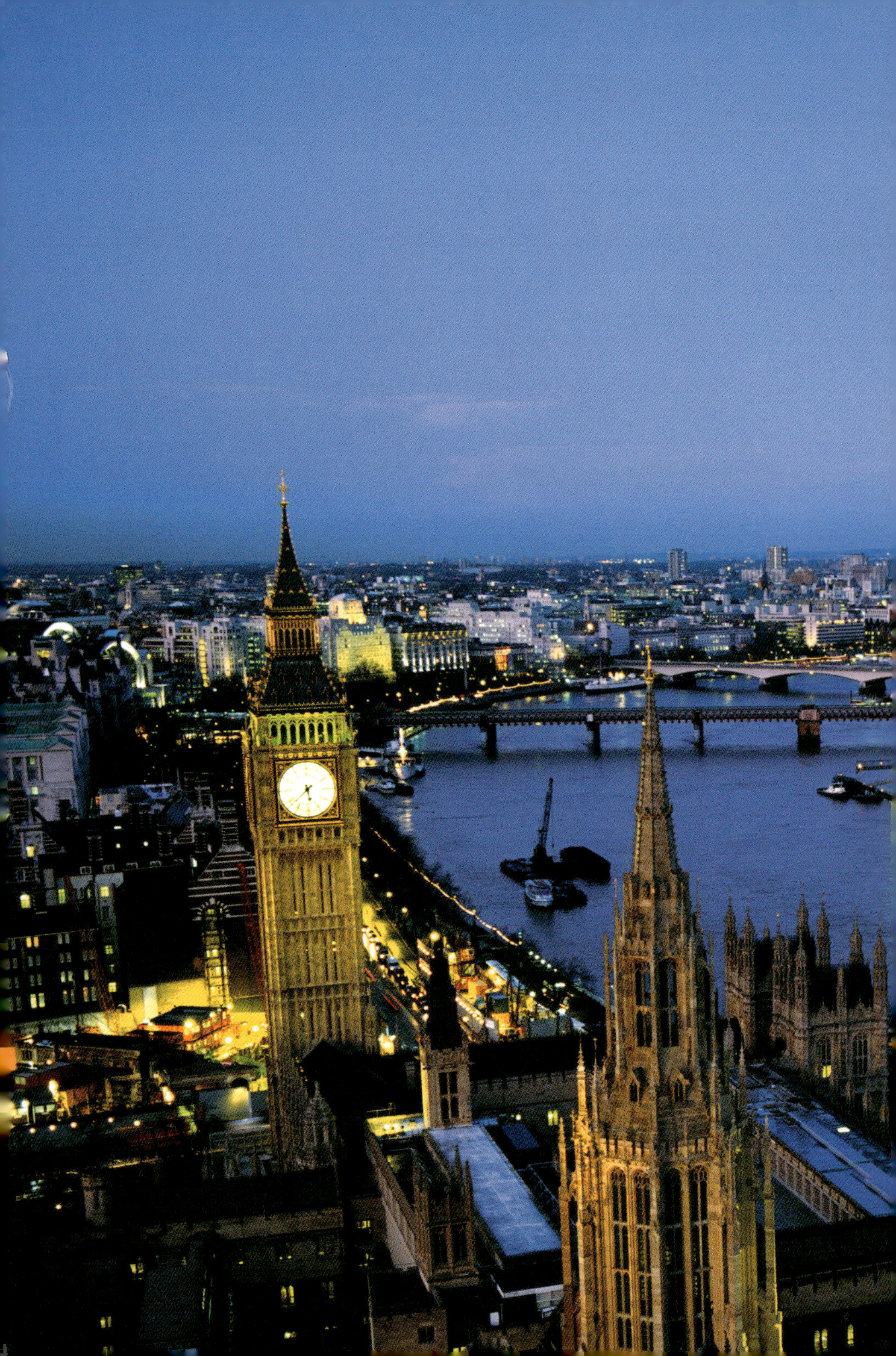

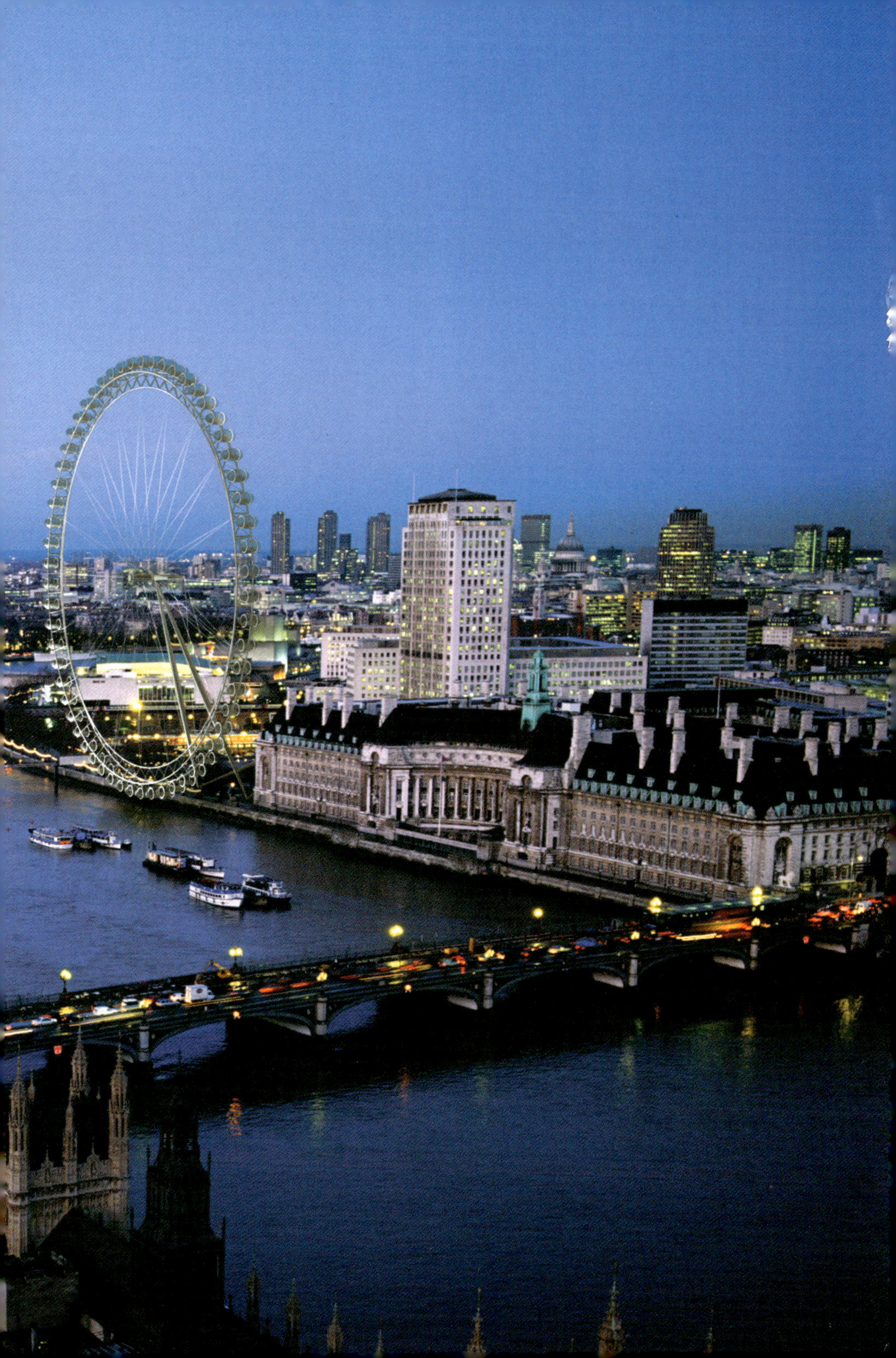

hd
fast forward

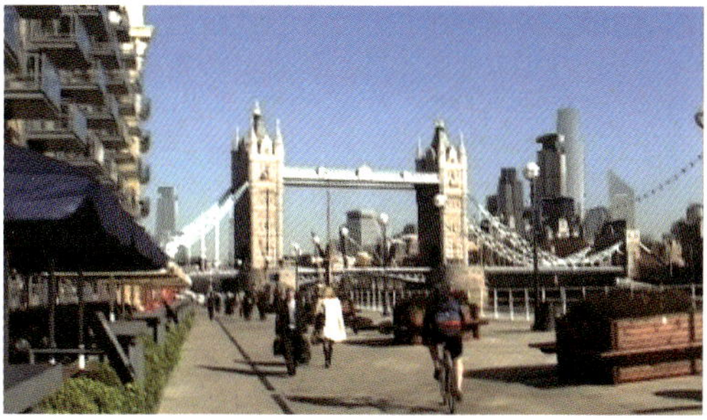

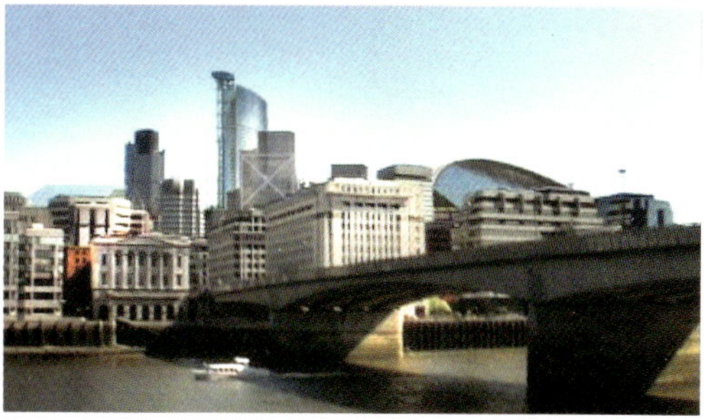

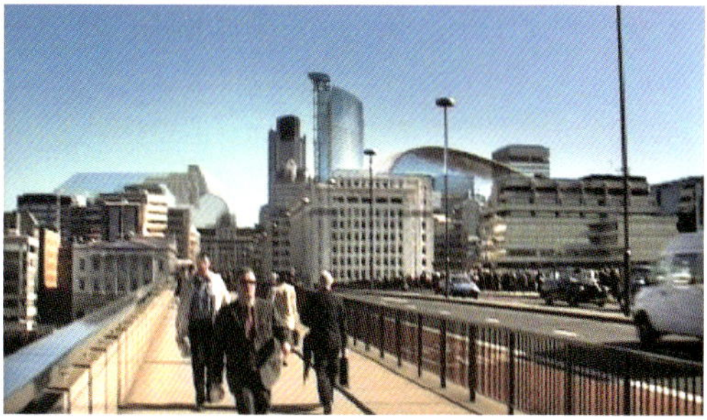

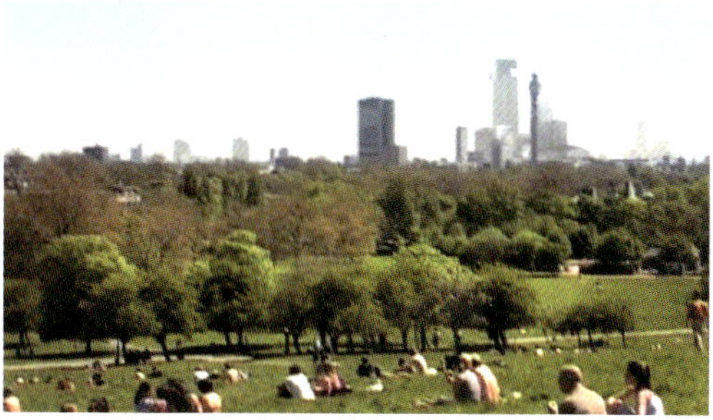

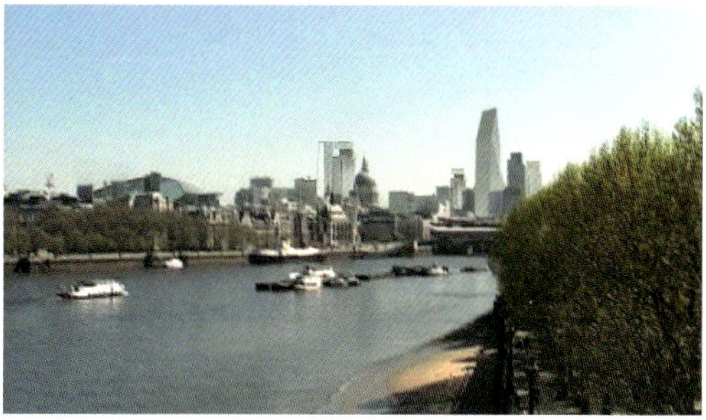

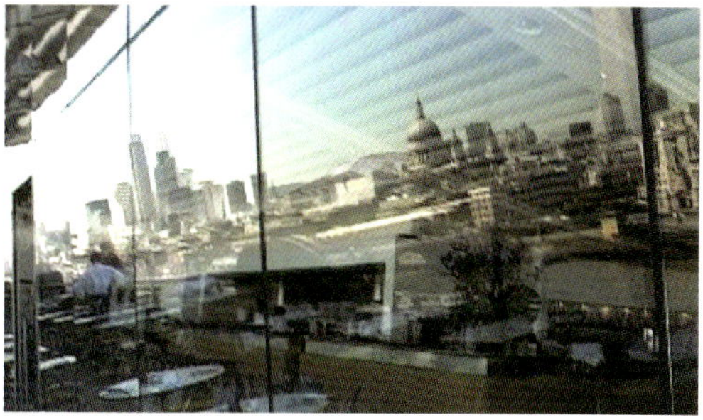

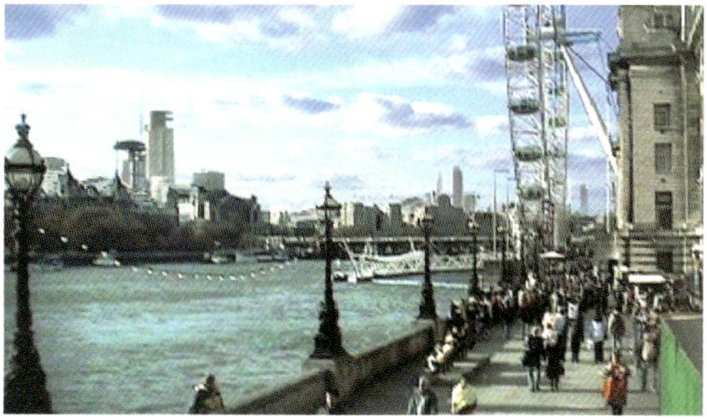

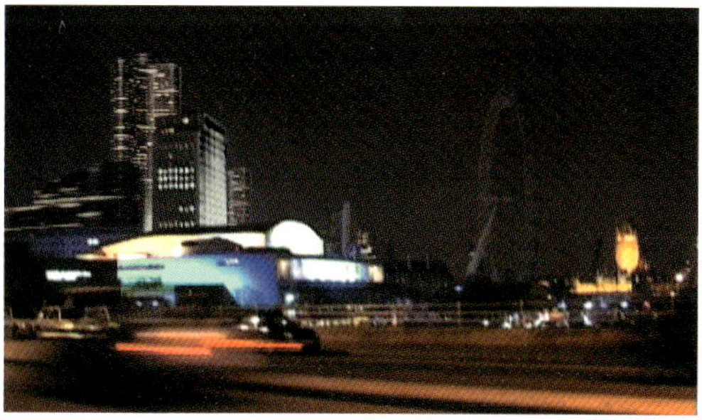

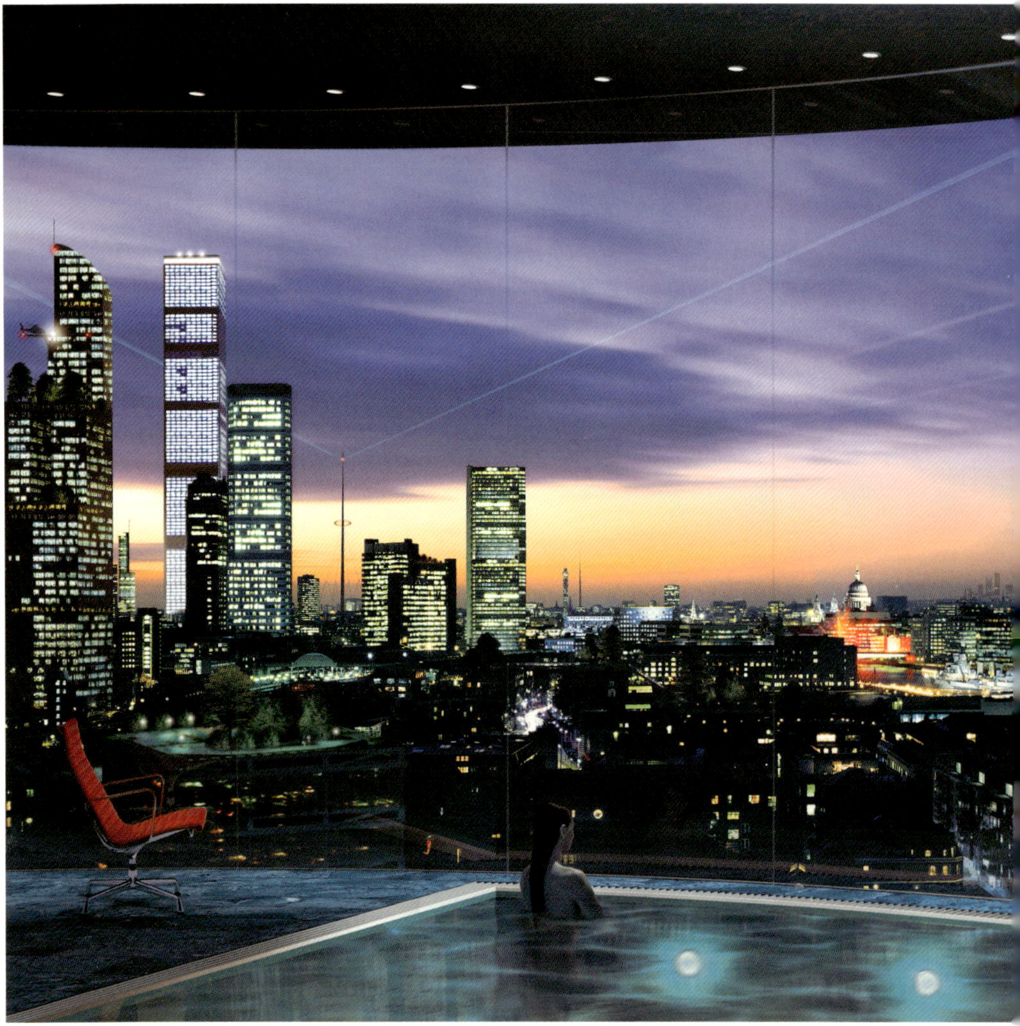

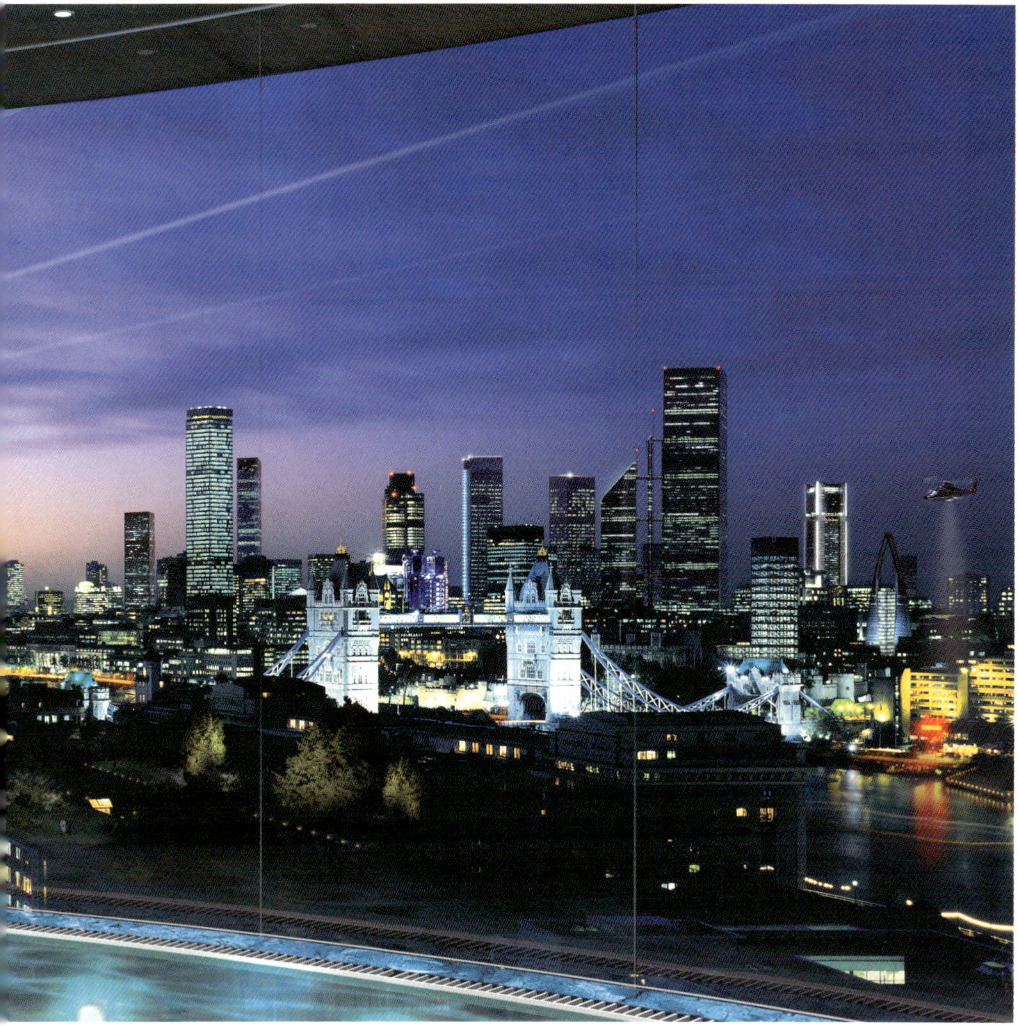

thank you

Rachel Arratoon
Matthew Austen
Arwen Banning
Andrew Beattie
Sue Beck
Lisa Bostock
Claire Brown
Ian Cartwright
Fleur Castell
Marie Chamillard
James Cheeseman
David Chisholm
Andrea Christelis
Neil Clark
George Constable
Noel da Costa
Ben Dale
Bim Daser
Alan Davidson
Anne Davidson
Ben Davies
Richard Davies
John Ding
James Eardley
Nacho Germade
Debbie Gibbs
Mark Glazier
Isabel Gonzaga Flores
Robert Gordon Clark
Jamie Green
Bob Hayes
Caite Healey
Jon Hey
Andrew Hilton
Simon Hindle
Owen Hui
Marika James

Mike Kane
Karl Kristiansen
Nigel Lang
Natasha LeCombe
Stephanie Levin
Deighton Lowe
Dan Macari
John Maclean
Dan Marsden
Fiona McDonald
Kath McDowell
Stuart Mills
Ed Mitchell
Alex Morris
Joy Nazzari
Hillary Neumayr
Eric Nixon
Flavio Ochoa
Steven Paul
Ximo Peres
Gill Pickles
Simone Poulton
Ana Prevel
Lewis Quinn
David Radford
Jo Robson
Stephen Sagi
Eleni Samara
Emma Scanlon
Julia Smith
Sophie Stirling
Jonny Stopford
Adam Taylor
Richard Watkins
Stephen Whitton
Tony Wilson
Nick Wood